The Uniqueness of Western Law
A REACTIONARY MANIFESTO

RICHARD STOREY

The UNIQUENESS of WESTERN LAW

A Reactionary Manifesto

ARKTOS
LONDON 2019

Copyright © 2019 by Arktos Media Ltd.

All rights reserved. No part of this book may be reproduced or utilized in any form or by any means (whether electronic or mechanical), including photocopying, recording or by any information storage and retrieval system, without permission in writing from the publisher.

ISBN	978-1-912975-03-7 (Softcover)
	978-1-912975-04-4 (Ebook)
EDITING, COVER AND LAYOUT	John Bruce Leonard

 Arktos.com   fb.com/Arktos    @arktosmedia   arktosmedia

CONTENTS

Introduction ... 1

PART ONE: NATURAL LAW

1. Libertarianism Is Only a Theory of Law ... 7
   — *A brief definition of libertarianism*
2. The Uniqueness of Western Law ... 9
   — *A study of the origins and history of natural law*
3. Estopping State Systems of Government ... 26
   — *A logical proof of the irrationality of state systems of government*
4. Libertarianism Is Going Medieval ... 35
   — *Predicting an increasingly reactionary libertarian movement*
5. Libertarianism Needs Nationalism (Not Statism) ... 46
   — *A libertarian argument for ethnic homogeneity*
6. Folk-Right Versus Multiculturalism ... 49
   — *An analysis of the superiority of blood-right citizenship (jus sanguinis)*

PART TWO: SOCIO-BIOLOGY

1. In Search of Non-White Philosophers ... 57
   — *A discussion of the minimal philosophical achievements outside of European civilisations*
2. Why There Are No Successful Black Nations... Yet! ... 61
   — *What principles should African nations take from the West?*
3. Why Libertarianism Is Unique to the 'West' ... 67
   — *What makes European civilisation different?*
4. Source of the Faustian West ... 77
   — *A hypothesis of the evolution of the unique culture of the West*
5. Is There a European Personality Type? ... 80
   — *An introduction to diverging European MBTI results*
6. Why Do Whites Choose White Guilt? ... 85
   — *Explaining the modern phenomenon of 'white guilt' in terms of the Faustian spirit of the West*

PART THREE: POLITICS

1. LIBERAL SUPREMACISM: TODAY'S WHITE MAN'S BURDEN — *How modern liberals impose their ideology worldwide, similar to the historical colonialists they decry* — 95
2. THE NEOCON SLAVE ETHIC — *Neo-conservatism does not represent the strength of Western civilisation* — 99
3. DEMOCRACY ISN'T WORKING — *A summary of the inferiority of the presently popular system of state government in the world* — 102
4. EUROPEANS WANT HUNGARY, NOT SWEDEN — *The stats have spoken* — 107
5. WHY THE WEST CAN'T UNITE AGAINST TERRORISM — *The consequences of abandoning Christianity* — 111
6. THE CORRELATION BETWEEN STATE GROWTH AND MASS IRRESPONSIBILITY — *An argument for subsidiarity* — 116

PART FOUR: FAMILY

1. WHY WOMEN ARE THE UNFAIRER SEX — *Discussing a scientific study which shows men are more sociable* — 123
2. FOUR REASONS MY HOUSEWIFE IS AWESOME — *Celebrating the motherly, homemaking role of traditional women* — 126
3. HOW TO BE A GOOD FATHER — *The importance of the traditional father in fulfilling basic human needs* — 130
4. WHY FIGHTING IS GOOD FOR MEN AND BOYS — *Instilling pride, respect and hopefully responsibility the way nature intended* — 136

Addendum — Fifteen Steps to Restore the West — *139*
Afterword by **Ricardo Duchesne** — *141*
Bibliography — *149*
Index — *153*

ADVANCE PRAISE FOR
THE UNIQUENESS OF WESTERN LAW

'Readers of Richard Storey's *The Uniqueness of Western Law* won't like his book — they will either love it or loathe it! Almost every page of this book challenges the creeds of current liberal orthodoxies (its subtitle is "A Reactionary Manifesto") and does so in a concise and scholarly yet very readable, fashion. Storey's approach to his topic is one that many readers will never have considered before and therein lies one, but not the only one, of its particular virtues. Read this book and prepare to be either exhilarated, encouraged and fascinated or disturbed, angered and provoked. Either way, you won't be bored!'

— **Gerard Casey**, *MA, LL.M., Ph.D., D.Litt., Professor Emeritus, University College Dublin, and author of* Freedom's Progress? A History of Political Thought

'All too many libertarians misconstrue the philosophy they are explaining. Not Richard Storey. He correctly states that libertarianism is solely a theory of just law. This chapter alone is worth the entire cost of admission. As a contrarian myself, I take my hat off to this author for his fearlessness and bravery.'

— **Walter E. Block**, *Ph.D., Harold E. Wirth Eminent Scholar Endowed Chair and Professor of Economics, Loyola University New Orleans*

'With its wide-ranging, yet easy to follow arguments, Richard Storey's Manifesto makes a compelling case for a conscientious libertarianism, rooted in the basic idea of the Western philosophical and Christian tradition, viz. that there is a freedom-promoting principle of order ("a natural law") of the world. It is a law that reveals itself in that most specifically human activity: raising and answering questions, arguing with each other, appealing to one another's conscience of our common humanity. Elucidating the real-world conditions that enable this conscientious search for order at all levels of human coexistence, Storey effectively destroys the caricature of libertarianism as "globalist market fundamentalism" that became prominent in the Cold War era.'

— **Frank van Dun**, *Ph.D., Dr.Jur., Senior lecturer Philosophy of Law at the University of Ghent*

For my Mother.
Thank you for teaching me loyalty.

INTRODUCTION

THE FOLLOWING MANIFESTO IS PRESENTED as a collection of articles, both popular and academic in style. These were published between 2016 and 2017 — a time of significant political change across the Western world. With the rise of nationalism, especially Christian nationalism, in the *Visegrád* Four and in Austria; with Brexit and the Catalonian struggle for peaceful secession in the EU; and with the election of nationalistic bombast in the form of Donald Trump in the US, etc., this has been a time for reflection on the history of the West, and consideration for its future.

During this time, my own journey has led me to study and reflect on my libertarian beliefs regarding law/politics and their exclusively Western character and point of origin. My greatest influences in producing these articles have been Ricardo Duchesne, professor of historical sociology at the University of New Brunswick in Canada, and Professor Frank van Dun, a natural law theorist associated with the University of Ghent in Belgium.

Prof. Duchesne has produced monumental work on the origins of Western civilisation in the culture of the Indo-European peoples who came to dominate and populate Europe. I find his theory to be superior and, as such, I shamelessly quote from his work throughout my articles. What's more, his writing sheds invaluable light on my research regarding the origins of Western law, libertarian values and institutions. His influence gave me a newfound respect for the Middle Ages and the world and order from which Western civilisation was built, as well as a guilt-free respect for both genetic *and* environmental factors in the development of unique cultures.

Prof. van Dun in turn helped me to understand the importance of Christendom in preserving and developing the libertarian system of natural law and social values, on the wealth of which we are still dependent today. Moreover, he was crucial in teaching me *the nemesis* of this order — modernism, specifically in the form of hyper- or Lutheran individualism.

Naturally, my concerns about the future of Western civilisation were not limited to historic causes of decline. The reason for the contemporary rise of nationalism in Western countries has been mass immigration from Third World countries into the West, and I have similarly been moved by my realisation that such political decisions would be absolutely destructive of Western civilisation for numerous socio-biological reasons. Moreover these are not simply missteps on the part of benevolent public servants (or at least of public servants who wish to seem benevolent), who have been misguided by the status quo of civic (rather than ethnic) nationalism or other liberal democratic values. Rather, these are deliberate acts, motivated by leftist ideologies which are dead set against the principles of natural law and justice and the hierarchical natural order — everything I have come to love about my dying civilisation.

The summary of my conclusions is that European civilisations have developed unique cultures and systems of law, and that to be preserved, they require: a return to the stateless, natural orders of the past; a respect for the importance of ethnic and cultural homogeneity in producing high-trust societies; and the powerful, personalistic cultural technology of Christianity. All alternatives are systems of disorder which, I argue, have not and cannot benefit or sustain the West as a civilisation.

What do I mean when I call this book a 'reactionary manifesto'? Am I referring to some sort of neo-reactionary traditionalism? Not exactly. Simply put, it is my hope that this book will help inspire restorative and secessionist movements, and the formation of self-governing communities across the West, especially those which strive to preserve Christendom. The audience I wish to inspire with this goal is perfectly identified by Prof. Hans-Hermann Hoppe:

> White married Christian couples with children, in particular if they belong also to the class of tax-*payers* (rather than tax-consumers), and everyone

most closely resembling or aspiring to this standard form of social order and organization can be realistically expected to be the most receptive audience of the libertarian message. [1]

I believe the most sensible option for the preservation of Western civilisation is the establishment of such bright 'cities on a hill' — shining examples or, at least, beacons of the core, historic values of our civilisation; and I believe the above group is the only one which can realistically accomplish this task. I hope this short book will convince you, the reader, of the same.

---

1 Hoppe, H. (2017). 'Libertarianism and the Alt-Right. In Search of a Libertarian Strategy for Social Change', speech delivered at the 12th annual meeting of the *Property and Freedom Society* in Bodrum, Turkey, on September 17, 2017; https://misesuk.org/2017/10/20/libertarianism-and-the-alt-right-hoppe-speech-2017/ (29/12/2017).

Part One
NATURAL LAW

Chapter 1

Libertarianism Is Only a Theory of Law

I AM TIRED OF BOTH LIBERTARIANS and their critics misrepresenting my beloved libertarianism by insisting that I am party to some sort of cult which teaches that some unspecified deity has written the non-aggression principle on tablets of stone. I have lost count of the number of times I have had to parrot the most notable libertarian scholars: libertarianism is just a theory of law; it is not an entire ethical system, complete with cultural mores, which *must* be imposed on everyone. As Lew Rockwell put it, 'Libertarianism is concerned with the use of violence in society. That is all. It is not anything else. It is not feminism. It is not egalitarianism… It has nothing to say about aesthetics. It has nothing to say about religion or race or nationality or sexual orientation.'

So when people dismiss libertarianism because certain libertarians are cultural Marxists, they do so out of ignorance. Libertarianism has a deontological attitude towards law; that is, in order for there to be certainty and security of private property rights, there must be the rule of law rather than the rule of legislators, and no man must be above the law. The only sense in which libertarians are egalitarian is that they think the law should apply equally to everyone in a given group—but this is equity and not egalitarianism.

This is the great Western heritage. It does not originate with the Anglo-Saxons or the ancient Greeks *per se*, but rather with the libertarian and egalitarian aristocracies of the Indo-Europeans from whom all the European civilisations are descended. Of course we recognise that not every civilisation *had to* establish the rule of law or the NAP (non-aggression principle) to function or to avoid a plague of locusts. Rather, libertarianism is part and parcel with the uniqueness of Western law and, therefore, the uniqueness of Western civilisation. But what is that law?

The unique Western attitude to law and its overwhelming success, according to Sinha, make it the fundamental and central trait of the West. The reason for making the law the king of kings lay in the higher degree of rationalism in the West with respect to other parts of the globe; if a law has to apply to all people in all situations, what social norms do just that? The only such 'right' we can determine is the negative right to be left alone in your person and property — private property rights. The nature of law, then, demands that *it* rule, lest we must submit to the unreliable whim of an individual or group which is legislated and imposed on us as if by divine power.

Naturally, the libertarian and egalitarian aristocracies of the Indo-Europeans produced civilisations which already acknowledged this, as the king could not violate the private property rights of another free man for fear of retribution from other powerful lords on the one hand, and the loss of honour, glory and respect from one's kinsmen on the other. Therefore, this rational and ruling law was not just discovered, but was studied and refined in its natural environment — the West.

So, the next time you think of dismissing libertarianism because you are repulsed by some open-borders supporter, some cucked feminist or someone who insists the world *must* fall before the NAP, remember that you can simply dismiss these people as ignorant without perforce dismissing libertarianism. What's more, if you understand that there is a difference between law and morality (the customs of a culture), and if you love Western civilisation and the rule of law, *you are* a libertarian!

Chapter 2

The Uniqueness of Western Law

> When accordingly it is inquired, whence is evil, it must first be inquired, what is evil, which is nothing else than corruption, either of the measure, or the form, or the order, that belong to nature.
>
> — St. Augustine

The study of Western Civilisation has been all but eradicated. This was no accident, but rather an aggressive policy of leftist academe which has used exclusionary tactics to dominate and pervert the culture and purpose of our universities since the 1960s and 70s.[1] But for us students, driven underground, Western history is the greatest treasure trove of almost every faculty. Not the least part of this treasure is natural law.

This unique philosophy of law so encapsulated the spirit of the West that the late Prof. Surya P. Sinha could describe law as 'the most central principle of [the] social organization' of Western civilisation alone. 'This fact explains that most…theories about law have issued from the Western culture.'[2] Prof. Sinha even declared *law itself* to be a non-universal phenomenon of the West, other civilisations developing little more than 'principles of moral life which are not law.'[3]

---

1 See Duchesne, R. (2011). *The Uniqueness of Western Civilization*, Leiden: Brill.
2 Sinha, S. P. (1993). *Jurisprudence Legal Philosophy: In a Nutshell*, St. Paul, Minn.: West Pub. Co., p. 8.
3 Sinha, S. P. (1995). 'Non-Universality of Law', *ARSP: Archiv Für Rechts- Und Sozialphilosophie / Archives for Philosophy of Law and Social Philosophy*, 81(2), pp. 185–214.

The story of natural law is a fascinating one; Prof. Ricardo Duchesne draws from decades of definitive scholarship on the uniqueness of the West to crystallise the 'essential message' from across the social sciences: 'the rise of the West is the story of the realization of humans who think of themselves as self-determining and therefore accept as authoritative only those norms and institutions that can be seen to be congenial with their awareness of themselves as free and rational agents.'[4] The origins of this law lie at the heart of Western civilisation, yet they are lost to history and shrouded in confusion. I would therefore like to clarify the environment in which natural law developed and the consequences of its loss.

I will discuss:

- The Indo-European, cultural origins of natural law;
- The Roman, statist confusion of natural law; and
- The Church's rightful title as successor in this tradition.

The Origins of Natural Law

I propose that natural law concepts germinated in the aristocratic culture of the Indo-European environment of ancient Greece and were nurtured by Christianity (a thoroughly Hellenistic religion); this explains why the Church found many similar concepts of kingship in the medieval Indo-European tribes of Northern Europe, particularly the rule of law and the right of resistance against tyrants. This allowed for the transition to and development of natural law, as well as the Church's creation of the first proper system of law in the world.

The classical natural law school of jurisprudence was concerned with the use of reason to discover the natural order of the world, particularly the world of men. This involved discovering universal rights which, by definition, cannot be alienated from anyone by anyone, thus rendering

---

4 Duchesne, R. (2011). *The Uniqueness of Western Civilization*, Leiden: Brill. p. 270.

everyone subject to this natural justice. Thus, the natural law rules as king of kings, rather than governing coercively as the legislated whim of a despot. But natural law was no accidental discovery; Prof. Sinha noted,

> the inquiring mind of the Greeks…failed to find an agreement among the priestly experts of the Middle East on fundamental questions [and so] they, in Ionia, began thinking about these questions themselves…. Instead, they used natural law to explain the phenomena.[5]

The universe then was considered ordered, perhaps even controllable — not the incomprehensible and whimsical sum of actions of untouchable gods. Natural phenomena had natural causes, according to pre-Socratic Thales of Miletus, and the same philosophy which saw the cosmos as a natural order applied to human societies too. This created environments less hospitable to those who would set themselves up as the sole source of social order; indeed, some of the Greek *poleis* were governed by the rule of law.[6]

Sinha concludes that the ancient Greek's desire to live 'for his own sake… marks the emergence of individualism.' However, he asserts that this individualistic rejection of oriental despots and unquestionable sage wisdom originates merely in the *environmental* factors of the Greek archipelago, in the shadow of the collapsed Mycenaean Kingdom.[7] Whilst such thinking is typical in today's academe, Prof. Duchesne's theory is more thorough:

> [T]he individualism of the Homeric heroes came originally from the Indo-European chieftains who took over the Greek mainland in the second millennium, and founded Mycenaean culture. [Thus] the primordial roots of

---

5 Ibid., p. 10.

6 Ober, J. (2015). *The Rise and Fall of Classical Greece*, Princeton University Press, Preface xv.

7 Sinha, S. P. (1993). *Jurisprudence Legal Philosophy: In a Nutshell*, St. Paul, Minn.: West Pub. Co., p. 8.

Western uniqueness must be traced back to the aristocratic warlike culture of the Indo-European speakers who spread throughout Europe during the 4th and 3rd millennium [B.C.].[8]

The uniqueness of the Indo-European egalitarian aristocracy was the freedom (and even encouragement) of individuals to strive for personal recognition — a Nietzschean 'restless ethos' in which berserkers flaunted their fearlessness in combat to earn respect and nobility.[9] The aristocracy (from the Greek word for excellent or virtuous being — '*aristos*') were thus the nobles of a society whose virtues were martial and masculine, as evidenced by the brotherhoods/war-bands of free men. The individualistic nature of these '*free* aristocrats' was not that of 'an autocrat who treats the upper classes as unequal servants but as "peers" who exist in a spirit of equality as warriors of noble birth.'[10]

Naturally, the mainspring of Western Civilisation's concern for liberty was the Indo-European culture of self-asserting, audacious individuals who continually competed against whomever would create a territorial monopoly of judicial power, thereby keeping not just despotic rule but any state-creating activity at bay. It was the inheritance of this ethos which caused the ancient Greeks to see the Oriental practice of prostration before the 'Great King' as 'symbolic confirmation of the great divergence between Eastern and Hellenic notions of individualism and political authority.'[11] Most significant, however, was the recounting of the individual heroic deeds of the *aristos* by the priestly class.

In depicting heroic deeds, the Indo-European spirit was internalised by the intellectual class of priests. This produced a highly competitive philosophical environment — 'the miracle of Greece' — which drove the *aristos* to greater feats of rational self-mastery, as Prof. Duchesne expounds:

---

8   Duchesne, R. (2011). *The Uniqueness of Western Civilization*, Leiden: Brill, p. 344.
9   Ibid., p. 368.
10 Ibid., pp. 372–373.
11 Ibid., p. 380.

> From Homer on, new standards of *arête* [virtue] began to evolve away from a strictly martial conception. Odysseus, the central character of the *Odyssey*, is seen to create meaning in his life not by risking his life in battles, but in his roles of spouse, parent, and joyful companion to his friends....
>
> The ultimate basis of Greek civic and cultural life was the aristocratic ethos of individualism and competitive conflict which pervaded IE culture. Ionian literature was far from the world of berserkers but it was nonetheless just as intensively competitive. New works of drama, philosophy, and music were expounded in the first-person form as an adversarial or athletic contest in the pursuit of truth... The search for the truth was a free-for-all with each philosopher competing for intellectual prestige in a polemical tone that sought to discredit the theories of others while promoting one's own.[12]

So, the Western concept of virtue (from *virtus*, the Roman, aristocratic concept of manliness) evolved from attributes associated with martial valour to those of the rational and civil man. In contrast to the violent hubris of Achilles, a new virtue emerged — '*Sophrosyne*, referring to moderation or self-restraint'.

> This virtue of moderation, it is argued, was suitable to the life of democratic discussion in the polis, which required self-control and 'sound mind.' This new virtue challenged the elitist view of the heroic age as a time when the social order was under the spell of mighty and turbulent aristocrats thirsting for glory and plunder without consideration for the pain and hardship they brought onto the world.[13]

Basically, the Greeks internalised the restless, conquering Indo-European spirit; philosophy and poetry began to depict their inner battles as well as outer. High competition in understanding the complexity of human reason, the psyche and society had begun. Rather than simply overpowering

---

12 Duchesne, R. (2011). *The Uniqueness of Western Civilization*, Leiden: Brill, pp. 450 & 452.

13 Ibid., p. 342.

the world around them, and even the gods, man turned inward to conquer himself, producing the self-civilising, trustworthy proto-gentleman who pursued Plato's four cardinal virtues — prudence, justice, temperance and courage.

The Roman Confusion of Natural Law

Natural law was famously developed further by the Roman lawyer, Cicero, but, whilst Roman civil law was mostly privately developed, the various Roman systems of government were not consistent examples of natural law in practice. Roman law developed primarily between the first century B.C. and the third century A.D. and comprised private and public law. Rothbard describes the difference between the two: 'Private law developed the theory of the absolute right of private property and of freedom of trade and contract. While Roman public law theoretically allowed state interference in the life of the citizen, there was little such interference in the late republic and early empire.' Since, as Prof. Jenő Szmodis notes, this 'duality of legal positivism versus natural law... is not known so sharply in other legal cultures,' the question arises: how did these two conflicting systems of governance develop together, as one legal system, in Rome, but not elsewhere in Europe?

The founding of Roman law was influenced by the ethnically Eastern Etruscans,[14] whose religion possessed typical Levantine attributes:

> The Roman formalistic and fatalistic view could not originate from...Indo-European religion...because Diaus-Pitar (Zeus-Iuppiter) represented an

---

14 The Near Eastern and non-Indo-European origin of the Etruscans, noted by Herodotus, has been well-attested by the genetic data. Nicholas Wade notes the largest studies of mtDNA indicate a Lydian, non-Indo-European origin, 'closest to Palestinians and Syrians'; furthermore, the DNA of their cattle comport with these findings, also having their origin in the Near East. — Wade, N. (2007). 'Origins of the Etruscans: Was Herodotus right?' *The New York Times*; http://www.nytimes.com/2007/04/03/health/03iht-snetrus.1.5127788.html?_r=0 (04/05/2016).

active force. However we know Etruscans respected highly the power of the Fate, and their oracles prophesied among others the decline of Etruscans themselves by strictly determined processes.[15]

A submissive, fatalist acceptance of the positivistic legislation of a state power was of course not the habit of Indo-European peoples. Equilibrium formed between public and private law, between the patrician rulers, influenced heavily by the Etruscans, and the mostly Latin and Greek population:

> The patrician law involved and preserved a fatalistic-formalistic morale, but the ideas about justice remained in non-formal condition in the plebeian cultural area. For example, Roman law only developed the concept of equity through the influence of the Indo-European Latins and the Greeks.[16]

The greatest evidence of this is the development of the Twelve Tables (*Leges Duodecim Tabularum*), the legislation which founded Roman law in the Republic (450–449 B.C.). After the expulsion of the last king of Rome, a Republic governed by magistrates was established by patrician rulers who denied the plebeian class access to the magistracy. According to Roman tradition, after a long social struggle between the two, with threats of secession by the plebeians, the Twelve Tables were produced. These visibly contained two influences: the Etruscan, ritualistic influence continued by the patrician class, i.e. various rituals required for certain formal transactions; and the desire to ensure that private property rights remained essentially unmolested, which was the main thrust of its diverse and disorganised content, revealing the influence of the natural-law style of thinking of the predominantly Indo-European plebeian class. So, public

---

15 Szmodis, J. (2011). 'On Law, History and Philosophy'. *Sectio Juridica et Politica*, Miskolc, Tomus XXIX/1, pp. 119—140. (For greater detail on the direct descent of Roman Law from the Etruscan system see also Szmodis, J. (2005) 'Reality of the Law: from the Etruscan Religion to the Postmodern Theories of Law', Budapest: Kairosz.)

16 Ibid.

and private law developed as one mixed legal system; as in Greece, private rights only had force under the auspices of the public law, yet there was no direct-governance undertaken by *all* free men. Of course, it may be countered that, in Roman history, the State interfered to a minimal degree in private disputes and private courts thus provided the required judicial services for resolution despite the State's legislative powers, as expounded by philosopher and lawyer, Bruno Leoni:

> A large part of the Roman rules of law was not due to any legislative process whatever. Private Roman law…was kept practically beyond the reach of legislators during most of the long history of the Roman Republic and the Empire… Statutory law for the Romans was mainly constitutional law or administrative law (and also criminal law), only indirectly relating to the private life and private business of the citizens.[17]

Nevertheless, as Prof. Hans-Hermann Hoppe predicts, in such circumstances,

> the definition of property and protection will be altered continually and the range of jurisdiction expanded to the government's advantage…[and] eternal and immutable law that must be *discovered* will disappear and be replaced by the idea of law as legislation — as flexible state-*made* law.[18]

This is precisely what happened in the later development of Roman law and through the later history of Western law, as influenced by it. During what is called 'The Crisis of the Third Century', the over-militarised Roman economy was weakened through donatives to a conditionally loyal and expansive army. Prof. Joseph R. Peden explains the deterioration of individual liberties during this period, as the public law expanded to extort greater taxes from the people, encroaching more heavily on citizens'

---

17   Leoni, B. (1991). *Freedom and the Law*, Indianapolis: Liberty Fund Inc., p. 83.
18   Hoppe, H. (2006). 'The Idea of a Private Law Society'; https://mises.org/library/idea-private-law-society (29/11/2017).

rights until they preferred life under the barbarians to the oppression of the imperial rule:

> Rome had basically a laissez-faire concept of state/economy relations. Except in emergencies, which were usually related to war... But now under the pressure of this need to pay the troops and under the pressure of inflation, the liberty of the people began to be seriously eroded — and very rapidly...
>
> The early 5th century Christian priest Salvian of Marseille wrote an account of why the Roman state was collapsing in the West.... [B]ecause it had denied the first premise of good government, which is justice to the people. By justice he meant a just system of taxation. Salvian tells us, and I don't think he's exaggerating, that one of the reasons why the Roman state collapsed in the 5th century was that the Roman people, the mass of the population, had but one wish after being captured by the barbarians: to never again fall under the rule of the Roman bureaucracy. In other words, the Roman state was the enemy; the barbarians were the liberators.... Rome continued to use an oppressive system of taxation in order to fill the coffers of the ruling bureaucrats and soldiers.[19]

Thus, St. Augustine could make this observation in the shadow of a moribund Western Rome:

> Justice being taken away, then, what are kingdoms but great robberies? For what are robberies themselves, but little kingdoms? The band itself is made up of men; it is ruled by the authority of a prince, it is knit together by the pact of the confederacy; the booty is divided by the law agreed on. If, by the admittance of abandoned men, this evil increases to such a degree that it holds places, fixes abodes, takes possession of cities, and subdues peoples, it assumes the more plainly the name of a kingdom, because the reality is now manifestly conferred on it, not by the removal of covetousness, but by the addition of impunity.[20]

---

19 Peden, J. R. (2009). 'Inflation and the Fall of the Roman Empire'; https://mises.org/library/inflation-and-fall-roman-empire (11/05/2016).

20 Augustine. *The City of God*, Ch. 4, 'How Like Kingdoms Without Justice are to Robberies'; http://www.newadvent.org/fathers/120104.htm (17/11/2017).

To explain why, as Lord Acton put it, 'Power tends to corrupt, and absolute power corrupts absolutely', would take an entire book. What's more, I'm not qualified to write it. But we can conclude, as Prof. Frank van Dun does, that either natural law rules, or some ideologue — either there is natural order, or unnatural disorder/chaos.

The word 'law' has Germanic roots and essentially means order. When we speak of a natural law we are thus talking about the natural order of rational agents with free will, in the same sense as Aristotle. Likewise, justice simply meant respect for this natural order and agreement between similarly natural persons. Today, however, law and justice are understood as being synonymous with state legislation and consequent legality.

> All of this goes under the academic label of 'positive law', which covers any one of the many particular imposed ("posited") systems of regulation by legal rules that we find in various politically organized societies.... Justice, then, is only an accidental and often marginal concern of the state. On the other hand, legality or conformity to the rules it imposes or wants to be obeyed is its central concern. (The word 'legality' derives from the Latin *lex*, which denotes a general command issued by a public authority, which originally was a military authority.)...
>
> The positive law is not the natural order of the human world. It is the artificial order that some powerful people (individuals and groups) in a particular society currently try to impose on others. It is an order, not of relations among human persons as such, but of relations among social positions, roles and functions. Thus the positive law of a particular country tells us what powers, immunities, rights, duties, claims and liabilities legally attach to the social positions, roles and functions of a general, a minister, a representative of the people, a citizen, a registered alien, a pensioner, a police man, and so on. In the same way, the rules of chess tell us what a king, queen, knight, pawn or other piece is or can or cannot do.[21]

Whilst not necessarily answering why power corrupts, we might at least

---

21 Van Dun, F. 'Natural Law'; http://users.ugent.be/~frvandun/Texts/Logica/Natural Law.htm (28/10/2017).

conclude that positive law is an excuse to use natural persons as a means to achieve ends which may have nothing to do with the natural order of the human world. If, as Prof. Duchesne concluded, 'the West is the story of the realization of humans who think of themselves as self-determining and therefore accept as authoritative only those norms and institutions that can be seen to be congenial with their awareness of themselves as free and rational agents', it is clear then why such a civilisation developed natural law.

Christianity Takes Up the Torch of Hellenistic Natural Law

The notion that the same rules apply to all men later found a home with the kings of Northern Europe. These tribes still possessed that Indo-European culture of the rule of an, albeit, customary law and the right to resist tyrants, with kings being answerable to the rulings of another lord's court. Therefore, the European Christendom of the Middle Ages presented a rather unique situation in which there was no state *per se*. This continued throughout the period primarily because natural law teachings of the Church largely comported with and developed the customary laws of the Germanic tribes, which, as Prof. Gerard Casey eloquently notes, always tend to the natural law anyway, being its 'local concretization'.[22]

In *Kingship and Law in the Middle Ages*, Fritz Kern explored the two major, similar concepts of law which the Church found among the Germanic tribes (the rule of law and the right to resist tyrants). The Church was able to exert a certain amount of influence in limiting the king's *dominium* but expanding his *imperium*, that is, obliging him to 'rule and defend this the realm which is vouchsafed to thee by God', as the German coronation order of the tenth century provides. Therefore, he was not to exercise any supposed superior rights, as a tyrant. Otherwise, the king

---

22 Casey, G. (2012). *Libertarian Anarchy: Against the State*, Continuum International Publishing Group, pp. 42 & 98.

was not consecrated or was excommunicated by the Church; likewise, he would not be considered a valid king by the people, but rather a criminal who could rightly face justice. Therefore, Kern concluded that a legally absolute king was impossible in the earlier Middle Ages.[23]

It is certainly the case that the aristocratic heritage of the Indo-European civilisations provided a plurality of judges, with the king being merely a first among equals, each lord's court exercising authority. Such an environment ensured (albeit imperfectly) competition in rationalising about resolutions to conflicts between parties and that no individual or group was beyond adjudication. Prof. Hoppe describes this non-exclusive territorial rule as an 'aristocratic natural order', when he expresses the attitude which allowed private systems of government and defied the creation of a state:

> The king is supposed to only apply law, not make it. And to assure this, the king will never be granted a monopoly on his position as judge.... [E]veryone remains free to select another judge, another noble, if he is dissatisfied with the king.... If he is found to make law, instead of just applying it, or if he is found to commit errors in the application of law, i.e., if he misconstrues, misrepresents, or falsifies the facts of a given case, his judgment stands open to be challenged in another noble court of justice, and he himself can there be held liable for his misjudgment. In short, the king may look like the head of a State, but he definitely is not a State but instead part of a natural, vertically and hierarchically structured and stratified social order: an aristocracy.[24]

As for the influence of the Church, whilst she had freedom to choose her own leaders, aristocrats would secure bishoprics etc. for family and friends, including the accompanying privileges and lands. Certainly, competition prevented the later rise of constitutional monarchs and subse-

---

23 Kern, F. (Tr. Chrimes S. B., 1968). *Kingship and Law in the Middle Ages*, London: Basil Blackwell, Intro. xix–xx.

24 Hoppe, H. (2015). *A Short History of Man: Progress and Decline*, Alabama: Mises Institute, p. 110.

quent states who sought greater revenue from the gradual monopolisation of judicial services.[25] But, as the emperor effectively hand-picked the pope, this allowed kings to corner the market on authority.

Pope Gregory VII understood this to be the source of corruption in the eleventh century and so, whilst still a cardinal-subdeacon, he established the College of Cardinals to elect the Pope; of course, they promptly elected him. The Gregorian Reform would furthermore establish judicial independence for the Church, producing the first proper *system* of law in the world — Canon law, built largely on natural law and various private law decisions from Roman and customary Germanic laws which accorded with it. This event would then secure similar self-determination for universities, guilds, merchants, entire cities etc.[26] Of course, the battle was not over; this was the start of the Investiture Controversy which commenced the struggle for superior authority between the Church and kings, later resulting in the Reformation, the rise of the nation-state, the Enlightenment, the French Revolution and the modern liberal-democracies, which are ubiquitous today.

We can conclude that the 'libertarian' aristocracy of the Indo-European civilisations produced and was, in turn, preserved by the philosophy of natural law into the feudal period, 'where no authority, not even the pope or the king, had complete political, religious, or intellectual jurisdiction.'[27] Although imperfect in many ways, natural law could be said to rule during this period in a way we cannot say of ancient Rome or the West today. So, the role of the Church in the widespread teaching of natural law (particularly as developed by the Scholastics) and the preservation of this traditional European system of rulership should not be underestimated; rather, it should be celebrated.

Nevertheless, it has been argued by various modernists, especially New

---

25 Benson, B. L. (1990). *The Enterprise of Law: Justice Without the State*, Pacific Research Institute for Public Policy, pp. 29-30.

26 See Berman, H. J. (1983). *Law and Revolution: The Formation of the Western Legal Tradition*, Harvard University Press.

27 Duchesne, R. (2011). *The Uniqueness of Western Civilization*. Leiden: Brill, p. 275.

Right thinkers, that pre-Christian Rome and the revival of its more anti-Christian features during the Renaissance and Enlightenment is more in keeping with the ancient culture and principles of European civilisation; what's more, that Christianity was essentially an alien, even subversive, Jewish ideological influence on European civilisation, and one which has been, at least in some ways, incompatible with the culture of Europeans.[28] On the contrary, as shown above, the Roman state was a divergence from Indo-European ideas of rulership in significant ways, such as the Greek experiments in freedom and the kings of the Germano-Celtic tribes. Now, I shall argue that Christianity is Hellenistic, a rightful successor of the natural law tradition, and, therefore, that it lies at the heart of Western civilisation.

In his article of the same name, Prof. Duchesne argues that 'Christianity is a Hellenistic Religion, and Western Civilization is Christian', following the scholarship of Prof. Martin Hengel—still the best source for the study of the Hellenistic period of Second Temple Judaism, from which Christianity emerged. He concluded that because of the interchange between Judaism and Hellenism, it is impossible to define Judaism as separate from it:

> It is too easily forgotten that in the time of Jesus Greek had already been established as a language for more than three hundred years and already had a long and varied history behind it.... The victorious Maccabaean revolt and the national and religious renewal associated with it had hardly changed anything in this respect.[29]

But, it was not simply popular language which was affected during this period. Remarking that Jerusalem had effectively become a Greek *polis* by 175 B.C., Prof. Hengel noted, 'It is evident here that the Hasmoneans did not really slow down the "process of Hellenization" in Palestinian Judaism,

---

28 For example, de Benoist, A. & Champetier, C. (2012). *Manifesto for a European Renaissance*, Arktos Media Ltd.

29 Hengel, M. (1989). *The 'Hellenization' of Judaea in the First Century After Christ*, SCM Press, pp. 7-8.

but in fact continued it as soon as they themselves came into power.'[30] The evidence for Greek being used as the *lingua franca* for trade, commerce and administration throughout Palestine has obviously increased since Prof. Hengel wrote those words, but he was still able to formulate an impressive list: Greek schools in Jerusalem as early as third century B.C.; bilingual coins (Herod produced purely Greek inscriptions on Jewish coins); borrowed Greek words to fill out the Jewish vocabulary (especially in Rabbinic literature); Greek architecture and public entertainment and Greek public inscriptions (some of the earliest evidence being in Jerusalem). Most significant, perhaps, is the development of individualism in the Second Temple Period literature as a result of this influence:

> This point of the discovery of the individual before God is probably the greatest gain of that encounter between the Jewish and Greek spirits which was so influential and at the same time so passionate. The certainty of the overcoming of death and the stress on the value of the individual unite in the glorification of the martyr. The Old Testament could not yet know the praise of the hero who dies for his ancestral city and its gods, but we find this praise of heroes all the more, say, in Greek poetry during the period of the Persian war. Although there are many reports in ancient Israel of the death of prophets and their faithfulness to YHWH, the prophets are never transformed into martyrs: in contrast to Greece, in Israel before the Hellenistic period (apart from the enigmatic text Isa.53) there is never any mention of a heroic "dying for".… That changes at a stroke in the Maccabean period.[31]

Prof. Hengel wasn't surprised, as Jerusalem 'was…a metropolis of international, world-wide significance, a great "attraction" in the literal sense, the centre of the inhabited world.'[32] Indeed, the number of dispersed Jewish pilgrims from all over the Roman Empire outnumbered the inhabitants

---

30 Hengel, M. (1980). *Jews, Greeks and Barbarians*, SCM Press, p. 117.
31 Hengel, M. (1989). *The 'Hellenization' of Judaea in the First Century After Christ*, SCM Press, p. 51.
32 Ibid., p. 11.

of Jerusalem and brought with them that foreign cultural influence. Jews of the Diaspora had been slaves in Greek homes, soldiers in Greek armies and even held worship services in Greek. 'The influence of Greek education and literature extends very much wider. We already find it in late Hebrew and Aramaic literature, for example in Koheleth, Ben Sira, Daniel or the Enoch writings.'[33] Notably, of course, St. Paul of Tarsus had received a Greek education which coloured his thought throughout his New Testament letters.

Many of the early Church, composed largely of Gentiles, intuited this strong connection with the natural law tradition of the Greeks. For example, St. Justin (early second century A.D.), in his proselytising *Dialogue with Trypho the Jew*, developed the identification of Christ as the Greek notion of the *logos* in the opening of John's Gospel. The *logos* is the ordering principle of the universe or 'Divine Reason', according to the Stoics. Therefore, St. Justin asserted that those Greeks who sought the natural order through reason had been led by God as much as the Old Testament figures, especially those who awaited the Messiah. '[Christ] is the Word [*logos*] of whom every race of men were partakers; and those who lived reasonably, are Christians, even though they have been thought atheists; as, among the Greeks, Socrates and Heraclitus, and men like them; and among the barbarians, Abraham, and Ananias'.

According to the data, St. Justin was right — there isn't simply a bridge between the natural law of Indo-European thought and Christianity, but, as Prof. Hengel observed, these movements are historically impossible to separate for definition. What's more, Christendom produced the personalistic form of individualism we know and take for granted as so typical of Western culture.[34]

---

33 Ibid., p. 21.
34 See Siedentop, L. (2014). *Inventing the Individual: The Origins of Western Liberalism*, Allen Lane.

Conclusion

It is hardly surprising that so many today complain that justice is blind. Our system of law is no longer based on the principles of Western natural law: legislators can make up the rules as they go, only recognising artificially determined persons for the achievement of an artificial order. Without any significant consensus to recognise principles of a natural order of human societies, there is nothing to mitigate the aforementioned process, and so the criteria of posited 'social justice' seem to be increasing exponentially in our time.

This is painfully and poetically clear when we consider the blind goddess of *Justitia*. Lady Justice is known today as a solitary figure. Long forgotten is her sister, *Prudentia*, with whom she was portrayed in times past. Alone and blind, the law is indeed an ass, for she doesn't have her sister to guide her toward any rationally observable order. Traditionally, however, the Church presented a universal moral framework for the West — one which reinforced the classical virtues, spurring Christians to strive for a more perfect world, with none other than prudence as the 'charioteer' of the classical or cardinal virtues.

The modern and especially post-modern mindset which has gripped the West has certainly blinded most of us to the objective principles which were the heart and soul of our civilisation; and without the heart of natural law establishing our families, communities and beyond, we can hardly be surprised that our civilisation is dead. At least we know the philosophy which gave it life and which could yet revitalise it.

Chapter 3

Estopping State Systems of Government

Introduction

THE STATE, BEING A JUDICIAL monopolist, is an irrational system of government because of the self-contradictory violation of private property rights required to establish or maintain it. Praxeological jurisprudence and the doctrine of dialogical estoppel provide the rational framework to show that, where there is incentive for rational consistency in the law, estopping the activities of state government and employing private judicial services is the only rationally viable option. The state, *qua* adjudicator of and/or party to civil disputes, seeks to protect private property rights, yet it must violate these rights to maintain its territorial monopoly; therefore, it cannot rationally claim a right to prevent competitors providing judicial services or delegitimise any act by private courts to estop state activities. This would necessarily result in a performative contradiction — a rights-violating rights protector is a contradiction in terms. Only private systems of governance, that is, private courts enforcing private law through *voluntary* interactions, can be consistent with the presuppositions of argumentation.

The conventional definition of a 'state' is a person or group maintaining a territorial monopoly of ultimate decision-making and, so, ultimate adjudicative power, even in disputes involving itself. As Hans-Hermann Hoppe put it, the state 'allows no appeal above and beyond itself. Furthermore, the state is an agency that exercises a territorial monopoly of taxation. That is, it is an agency that unilaterally fixes the price private citizens must pay for its provision of law and order.'[1] This definition applies equally to states which exercise a separation of powers; an independent judiciary, for instance, is nevertheless an interdependent body of state government, exercising a monopoly of judicial services and receiving its funding from the same source of taxation.

This article was inspired by Frank van Dun's example of a stereotypically crooked judge:

> An official condemns a man to the gallows, having heard only the arguments and witnesses of the prosecution and having denied the accused the right to defend himself. There is not a whiff of dialectical contradiction there as long as the official places himself in the realm of brute force or cunning manipulation, demonstrating by words or actions that he does not intend to justify his action. However, he would dialectically contradict himself if he were to go on to say that he has rendered justice and spoken truly as required by the ethics of argumentation.[2]

For identical reasons, the state, by definition, cannot engage in an adjudicative role without contradicting itself — the state's *aggressive* imposition of judicial monopoly is inconsistent with its role as a judge in civil disputes. Thus, the state, as a result of its irrational nature, is always a crooked judge.

Instead, Hoppe has proposed the creation of competition in the market of judicial services as a method to establish a free society, that is, a 'private law society'.[3] Hoppe's social theory builds on the logical science

---

[1] Hoppe, H. (2006). 'The Idea of a Private Law Society'; https://mises.org/library/idea-private-law-society (30/02/2016).

[2] Van Dun, F. (2009). 'Argumentation Ethics and The Philosophy of Freedom', *Libertarian Papers*, 1, 19.

[3] Hoppe, H. (2006). 'The Idea of a Private Law Society'; https://mises.org/library/idea-private-law-society (30/02/2016).

of praxeology by applying it to human interaction in argumentation ethics; this has, in turn, been applied in the field of jurisprudence by Stephan Kinsella to develop the doctrine of dialogical estoppel. A summation of the presuppositions of argumentation, particularly private property rights, is provided; further to this, it will be shown that the state commits a performative contradiction in the aggressive establishment of a territorial monopoly of ultimate decision-making power and, therefore, of judicial and legislative authority. Thus, the doctrine of dialogical estoppel can theoretically be applied to estop the state's actions in a private court.

For a full treatment of the foundations of praxeological jurisprudence and the use of praxeology to reformulate key legal concepts and the analysis of legal-theory controversies, see Konrad Graf's article, 'Action-Based Jurisprudence: Praxeological Legal Theory in Relation to Economic Theory, Ethics, and Legal Practice'.[4] Praxeological jurisprudence is not a theory of natural law *per se*, i.e. deontological ethical principles which people can discover through reason and *ought to* apply to their own decisions and acts. Praxeological jurisprudence is concerned with determining *a priori* what the presuppositions of argumentation *are*. Nevertheless, it is rationally objective and, thus, opposed to legal positivism; as such, it is described as 'an emerging school of jurisprudence related to, but distinct from, natural law'.[5] It is therefore important to note that praxeological jurisprudence is distinct, especially from the positivist schools of jurisprudence; these emphasise law as a social construct, that is, rules which must be legislated by the judiciary and legislature of a state system of government. Graf's article also provides a fuller treatment of this and the distinction between law and morality. In light of this key distinction between legal and ethical realms, the aim of this article is not to declare that all state systems of government *should* be abolished *because* they are irrational; states are of course feasible and are the overwhelmingly domi-

---

4   Graf, K. 'Action-Based Jurisprudence: Praxeological Legal Theory in Relation to Economic Theory, Ethics, and Legal Practice', *Libertarian Papers*, 3, 19 (2011).
5   Ibid.

nant form of government in human societies.

This article rather concludes that, by default, a restoration of private law, through competing, private systems of government (e.g. theoretical Hoppean private law societies, the medieval system of ecclesiastical courts etc.) is the only logically valid option for providing judicial services. It is not the intention of this article to make any assertions regarding sovereignty or to show that private governance is more efficient or 'works better' than state governance in any utilitarian sense. For such studies, please refer to Bruce L. Benson's *The Enterprise of Law: Justice Without the State* (1990) and Edward P. Stringham's *Private Governance: Creating Order in Economic and Social Life* (2015).

Praxeological Jurisprudence and the Irrationality of Judicial Monopoly

It shall now be shown that state judicial monopolies are irrational. First, it must be shown that an individual who violates private property rights can be lawfully and incontestably estopped from claiming the right to do so by any private court. Additionally, the representatives of the state can equally be estopped from engaging in the adjudication of legal disputes for this very reason.

Foundational to Hoppe's social theory is Ludwig von Mises' *a priori* of human action, otherwise known as the action axiom. Mises determined a universally valid foundation for economics by stripping the concept of action down to a bare minimum: agents act purposively by choosing means and ends. He concluded that the concept of purposeful human action is 'like those of logic and mathematics, *a priori*. They are not subject to verification or falsification on the ground of experience and facts.'[6] He therefore proposed that 'science — at least for the time being — must

---

6   Von Mises, L. (1998). *Human Action: Scholar's Edition*, Alabama: The Ludwig von Mises Institute, p. 32.

adopt a dualistic approach...[taking] into account the fact that we do not know how external events—physical, chemical, and physiological—affect human thoughts, ideas, and judgments of value.' Thus, Mises' epistemological dualism proposed that the empirical social and natural scientific methods must be used in tandem with the logic of human thought and action—'praxeology'.[7]

Hoppe has expanded praxeology into the area of ethics (human *inter*action) with the development of argumentation ethics.[8] He has shown that the human act of engaging in non-aggressive disputes, with the use of discourse, presupposes certain norms, especially self-ownership and private property:

> Argumentation does not consist of free-floating propositions but is a form of action requiring the employment of scarce means; and that the means which a person demonstrates as preferring by engaging in propositional exchanges are those of private property. For one thing, no one could possibly propose anything, and no one could become convinced of any proposition by argumentative means, if a person's right to make exclusive use of his physical body were not already presupposed. It is this recognition of each other's mutually exclusive control over one's own body which explains the distinctive character of propositional exchanges that, while one may disagree about what has been said, it is still possible to agree at least on the fact that there is disagreement. It is also obvious that such a property right to one's own body must be said to be justified *a priori*, for anyone who tried to justify any norm whatsoever would already have to presuppose the exclusive right of control over his body as a valid norm simply in order to say, "I propose such and such." Anyone disputing such a right would become caught up in a practical contradiction since arguing so would already imply acceptance of the very norm which he was disputing.[9]

---

7   Von Mises, L. (1957). *Theory and History*, New Haven: Yale University Press, p. 1.
8   Graf, K. 'Action-Based Jurisprudence: Praxeological Legal Theory in Relation to Economic Theory, Ethics, and Legal Practice', *Libertarian Papers*, 3, 19 (2011).
9   Hoppe, H. (1993). *The Economics and Ethics Of Private Property*, Boston: Kluwer Academic Publishers, p. 342.

The brilliance of Hoppe's theory is that, in the very act of arguing contrary to it, one demonstrates its validity. For example, to *argue* that violence is the best way to resolve a conflict is a performative contradiction. Focusing on the justification of private property rights through argumentation ethics, Hoppe writes:

> [I]t should be noted that if no one had the right to acquire and control anything except his own body…then we would all cease to exist and the problem of the justification of normative statements…simply would not exist. The existence of this problem is only possible because we are alive, and our existence is due to the fact that we do not, indeed *cannot*, accept a norm outlawing property in other scarce goods next and in addition to that of one's physical body. Hence, the right to acquire such goods must be assumed to exist.[10]

Kinsella has applied these norms with the observation that the common-law equitable doctrine of estoppel is, essentially, an intuitive application of Hoppe's theory of argumentation. Broadly, estoppel 'prevents or precludes someone from making a claim in a lawsuit that is inconsistent with his prior conduct'. As Kinsella explains,

> The basic insight behind this theory of rights is that a person cannot consistently object to being punished if he has himself initiated force. He is (dialogically) "estopped" from asserting the impropriety of the force used to punish him, because of his own coercive behavior. This theory also establishes the validity of the libertarian conception of rights as being strictly negative rights against aggression, the initiation of force.[11]

The significance of this development is the refining of the natural law school of jurisprudence, given its history of arbitrary and sometimes contradictory notions of what 'nature' is, towards a praxeological approach.

---

10 Ibid. p. 320.
11 Kinsella, N. S. (1996). 'Libertarian Theory of Punishment and Rights', a. *Loy. LAL Rev.*, 30, p. 607.

What Graf characterises more broadly as a distinct new action-based school of jurisprudence. As Hoppe notes, 'The praxeological approach solves this problem by recognizing that it is not the wider concept of human nature but the narrower one of propositional exchanges and argumentation which must serve as the starting point in deriving an ethic.'[12] For this reason, a praxeological approach towards jurisprudence provides universally applicable social norms, in contrast to the dominant positivistic schools of jurisprudence, which lack rational certainty, deriving law from arbitrary and subjective legislation. An adjudicator in a civil dispute can, therefore, make confident assertions when analysing the facts of any given case (the empirical data) in light of the incontestable private property rights which are implicitly accepted when parties engage in non-aggressive disputes.

According to the principle of dialogical estoppel, the state, as an agency which violently expropriates property, can be estopped by any private court from claiming a legal right to tax this property; only the party who is victim to such actions can claim any rights. In this way, the second function of a state (taxing), cannot be rationally legitimated through public law. Furthermore, a judge in disputes accepts the same presuppositions of argumentation as the disputants. Whilst dialogical estoppel requires that a judge also come to court with 'clean hands', i.e. consistent prior behaviour, the state must use aggression to maintain its position as a judicial monopolist. By *aggressively* 'outlawing' adjudicative services by other parties, the state can be rightly estopped from adjudicating in civil disputes. Also, the state cannot claim a right to prevent competitors from providing judicial services; as the state must resort to irrational and violent means to maintain this territorial monopoly of ultimate decision making, it cannot rationally declare illegal any act by private courts to estop these state activities and claim the right to avoid similar treatment. This necessarily results in a performative contradiction.

---

12 Hoppe, H. (1993). *The Economics and Ethics Of Private Property*, Boston: Kluwer Academic Publishers, p. 345.

The conventional wisdom regarding the state is: 'The same coercive power that allows [the state] to protect property rights and provide public safety also allows [the state] to confiscate private property and abuse the rights of their citizens.'[13] But this is erroneous. It is not that the state *either* protects *or* violates one's private property rights; in Hoppean language, before the state monopoly can produce the good of judicial service, it must first produce the bad of invasive violence, inconsistent with the justice it seeks to provide. Thus, the contradiction of the rights-violating rights protector.

Conclusion

The state, defined as a coercively taxing, territorial judicial monopolist, is indeed a 'crooked' judge. The state contradicts itself by seeking to aggressively maintain a monopoly of judicial services, contrary to the private property rights presupposed by the act of civil disputation. Only private systems of governance, that is, private courts enforcing private law, can be consistent with the presuppositions of argumentation, as these alone rely on non-coercive means of providing judicial services.

As to how this might be achieved, perhaps there are lessons to be learned from pre-modern Europe: Roman law was developed privately and medieval scholars of Catholic canon law were likewise influenced to develop their own comprehensive system of law and governance for the Church, an institution central to medieval culture, politics, and higher learning. This formed the basis of Civil law and was implemented across Europe. In the Common law tradition too, before the rise of states proper, a private system of law arose out of custom in which *imperium* was supposed to be the servant of *dominium*, sovereignty subordinate to property, the sovereign having the power to enforce, not to create the law. Here too, the Church played the role of the spiritual sword working with and keeping in check

---

13 Fukuyama, F. (2004). *State-Building: Governance and World Order in the Twenty-First Century*, London: Profile Books, p. 1.

the temporal sword of the state for the public good, ensuring that Natural Law was upheld.

As our understanding of Natural Law evolves, revisiting the systems which gave rise to Western law seems ever more pertinent. Could the irrationality of the state system of government thus be resolved through the empowerment of our national and cultural institutions, such as the Church, with the responsibility to privately develop the law that sovereigns are to enforce? Praxeological jurisprudence and the doctrine of dialogical estoppel provide the rational framework to accomplish this. Certainly, this would make for interesting further study.

Chapter 4

Libertarianism Is Going Medieval

I HAVE LONG BELIEVED THAT THE realisation of anarcho-capitalist principles would most resemble the stateless societies of medieval Europe. After all, there seems no other time or place in which such an ordered anarchy has existed, nor which warrants Rothbard's description of a 'gorgeous mosaic' of self-governing communities. Yet, most others have rather envisioned some future 'Ancapistani' sci-fi utopia — the aesthetics of *Blade Runner* tempered by the mild-mannered industriousness of *Star Trek*, perhaps. Now, however, it seems that many right-libertarians, disillusioned with such hyper-individualistic caricatures, are on the verge of agreeing with me; but how, and why?

You might be forgiven for assuming that the recent increase in identitarian political views across the West (in opposition to the now-dominant cultural Marxism in various institutional authorities) prompted this soul-searching. In fact, this was merely the catalyst. For example, Mises Institute President Jeff Deist's 'blood and soil' speech simply reaffirmed (and informally ratified) social principles which had been long-since developed in libertarian thought. Rothbard of course had identified the growing issue of hyper-individualism in right-libertarianism:

> Contemporary libertarians often assume, mistakenly, that individuals are bound to each other only by the nexus of market exchange. They forget that everyone is necessarily born into a family, a language, and a culture. Every person is born into one or several overlapping communities, usually

including an ethnic group, with specific values, cultures, religious beliefs, and traditions.[1]

Nevertheless, Rothbard was trapped in the same sort of modernist thinking which lends itself more to an incremental individualism rather than, say, the personalism of the Middle Ages. In his article, 'Left and Right: The Prospects for Liberty', Rothbard more or less equated the 'old order' with oriental despotism and implicitly accepted the Constitutional Republicanism of the US as a monumental milestone of liberty — a false assumption all too common among Americans. Rather, it fell to Prof. Hans-Hermann Hoppe to specifically identify and tackle the 'standard libertarian model of a community', i.e. 'neighbors living on adjacent…pieces of land owned in severalty', as 'too simplistic.' He instead presented the superiority of the natural order of kings and the hierarchical, aristocratic old order in his book, *Democracy — The God That Failed*, and in a brilliant essay, '*From Aristocracy To Monarchy To Democracy: A Tale of Moral and Economic Folly and Decay*':

> [N]eighborhoods have typically been proprietary or covenantal communities, founded and owned by a single proprietor who would 'lease' separate parts of the land under specified conditions to selected individuals. Originally, such covenants were based on kinship relations, with the role of the proprietor performed by the head of a family or clan… In modern times, characterized by massive population growth and a significant loss in the importance of kinship relations, this original libertarian model of a proprietary community has been replaced by new and familiar developments such as shopping malls and gated communities.[2]

This was an important step away from the 'purely contractual' rela-

---

1 Rothbard, M. (ed. 2014). 'A Libertarian View of Nationalism, Secession, and Ethnic Enclaves'; https://mises.org/blog/libertarian-view-nationalism-secession-and-ethnic-enclaves (29/10/2017).
2 Hoppe, H. (2001). *Democracy — The God That Failed: The Economics and Politics of Monarchy, Democracy and Natural Order*, Transaction Publishers, pp. 213–215.

tionships which comprise the individualism of the modern West and not just modern, liberal democratic states but also modern (contractarian and propertarian) libertarian thought. And it was on this more personalistic foundation that Deist could say,

> it remains true that civil society should be celebrated by libertarians at every turn. To believe otherwise is to ignore what humans actually want and actually do, which is create communities. There is a word for people who believe in nothing: not government, family, God, society, morality, or civilisation. And that word is nihilist, not libertarian.

I wonder whether, as well as adopting traditionalist views regarding the family, community and the natural rulership of kings and lords, many right-libertarians will likewise accept the important role of the Church in the development of Western civilisation, especially in developing and preserving natural law. Personally, I think it is inevitable.

Natural Law Libertarianism

What is libertarianism? Lew Rockwell, among others, has correctly identified it as a set of legal theories: 'Libertarianism is concerned with the use of violence in society. That is all. It is not anything else.'[3] In this cruel world of competition for scarce resources, we can only resolve disputes through violence, agreement or adjudication — the latter two being the prudent avoidance or conscientious use of violence. So we must go on to define what lawful violence is, i.e. what justice is.

We humans are social creatures who reciprocate and seek out prudent means to balance the achievement of our individual aims with group expectations. Thus, a natural order is established, minimising conflict over scarce resources in the achievement of said aims, within or even between

---

3   Rockwell, L. (2014). 'What Libertarianism Is, and Isn't'; https://www.lewrockwell.com/2014/03/lew-rockwell/what-libertarianism-is-and-isnt/ (29/10/2017).

groups. Needless to say, reckless violence is disorderly and disrupts this natural balance, and, indeed, customary systems of law always tend towards natural law so understood. However, many right-libertarians hesitate to refer to natural justice/law/order, regardless of how definitively the debate between Rawls and Nozick was won in favour of Nozick's natural rights. Yet, leftists of all shades continue to develop ideas regarding 'social justice', civil rights — all positively legislated by the state.

Libertarians fail to stand firm on the immovable rock of natural law, but they might refer to the negative 'right' of being left unmolested in one's person or property. It is, of course, true that this is the only universal and unconditional right we can identify, and one that is shamelessly negated by the torrent of positive legal rights imposed by states. Rothbard gives a humorous example of this:

> If I am sick unto death, and the only thing that will save my life is the touch of Henry Fonda's cool hand on my fevered brow, then all the same, I have no right to be given the touch of Henry Fonda's cool hand on my fevered brow. It would be frightfully nice of him to fly in from the West Coast to provide it. It would be less nice, though no doubt well meant, if my friends flew out to the West coast and brought Henry Fonda back with them. But I have no right at all against anybody that he should do this for me.[4]

But, simply identifying a 'right' isn't sufficient to challenge the self-legitimising Leviathan of the modern state. ' "Right," according to whom?' it is asked. So, the fundamental question is whether we understand law as something imposed or found. Is it primarily a matter of legislation or primarily a matter of jurisprudence? Is it a matter of 'applying' one or other theory of law/rights or a matter of preventing, solving or managing conflicts as well as one can? Sadly, many libertarians today would rather choose the former and, at most, adopt Rothbard's self-identification as a 'natural rightser'. For example, I believe most would declare something 'right' because it was signed as a deed,

---

4   Rothard, M. (2002). *The Ethics of Liberty*, New York University Press, p. 99.

regardless of how a judge might be able to interpret the past and current behaviour of the parties.

Prof. Frank van Dun rebukes this modern, contractarian view: '[A]narchocapitalism, in its Rothbardian form, stands or falls with its supposition that there is a natural order — a natural law — of the human world and that each human person has a place in that order that is delimited by his or her natural rights.'[5] Jurisprudence and equity must trump legalism, as they once did, when the Church defended a plurality of jurisdictions across medieval Europe under a voluntarily shared moral and cultural framework. Yet laymen and scholars, libertarian or not, recoil at the mention of natural law. Why?

The answer, it would seem, is that the dominant, materialist thinking in academe is suspicious of the historical connection that natural law theory has with the Church. Many are keen to reiterate 'Hume's law' — an 'is' doesn't make an 'ought' — i.e. just because humans and human societies are a certain way, doesn't mean humans *must* behave a certain way according to an objective system of law. But, echoing Prof. van Dun, Prof. Casey, notes that natural law is not synonymous with any 'divine command theory' and that the word 'natural' should make the normative function of natural law as obvious as it has been historically.[6]

So, in answer to the question, 'What is justice?' Prof. van Dun explains it is synonymous with the maintenance of the natural order of the human world:

> [T]he literal meaning of 'justice' (Latin: iustitia) is 'what is conducive to ius'. In other words, justice is what aims at the establishment of the condition in which people interact on the basis of mutual consent. Justice is respect for law in the sense of 'ius'. Justice does not imply respect for the laws (leges) that might be enforced by the authorities, except in those cases when they are genuine rules of law... [So, if] 'law' means order and not command, rule or

---

5   Van Dun, F. (2003). 'Natural Law. A Logical Analysis', *Etica & Politica / Ethics & Politics*, 2003, 2.
6   See Casey, G. (2012). *Libertarian Anarchy: Against the State*, Continuum International Publishing Group.

norm, 'natural law' is no longer a mystifying concept. It stands for the natural order of the human world… The question before us is: What is the natural law or order of the human world?[7]

Surely, any libertarian familiar with and fond of 'the NAP' or Hoppean social theory should readily identify as a natural law libertarian. Nevertheless, Rothbard's modernism kept him from asserting any *particular system* of natural law himself, despite defending the more rational principles of Thomistic natural law. It is no wonder then that he so celebrated Prof. Hoppe's value-free system of argumentation ethics in his article, 'Beyond Is and Ought': '[Hoppe] has managed to transcend the famous is/ought, fact/value dichotomy that has plagued philosophy since the days of the scholastics, and that had brought modern libertarianism into a tiresome deadlock.' Yet, argumentation ethics is simply a principle of natural law!

Prof. Hoppe's theory assumes a juristic, rather than a legalistic, perspective, as it focuses on the presuppositions made when an individual engages in some sort of rational discourse, rather than violence. To continue my truncated description of this theory, such an omission of violence *implies* that the principles of private property are necessarily acknowledged by the parties involved in rational discourse. This analysis of *behaviour* prompted Stephan Kinsella to identify argumentation ethics as, in practice, an application of the equitable (and therefore juristic) common law doctrine of estoppel.[8] According to *Black's Law Dictionary*, this doctrine 'precludes a man from alleging or from denying a certain fact or state of facts, in consequence of his previous allegation or denial *or conduct* or admission' (emphasis mine).

In this way, judges use jurisprudence to determine whether plaintiffs have acted 'in bad faith' with respect to a dispute; that is, 'those seeking equity must do equity' or 'equity must come with clean hands'. And, it should go without saying that the underlying principles of this common

---

7 Van Dun, F. 'Kritarchy'; https://americankritarchists.wordpress.com/article-by-frank-van-dun/ (29/10/2017).

8 Kinsella, Stephan. 'Punishment and Proportionality: the Estoppel Approach.' *Journal of Libertarian Studies*, 12, No. 1 (1996): 51–73.

law (*ius commune* or folk-right) were developed by bishops in Anglo-Saxon courts and sustained by later influences of those natural law elements of the Church's Canon law.

I have, myself, contributed to this study of what Konrad Graf calls 'praxeological jurisprudence', understanding it to be a normative refining of natural law.[9] But, upon discussing this subject with Prof. van Dun, who arrived at the same conclusions of argumentation ethics independently in the early 1980s (describing it as 'dialogue ethics'), he made it clear that the probable function of these doctrines has been to *reform* natural law away from the modernist, legalist or rights-centred view of today, back to its Medieval intent. Argumentation ethics is still well in the realm of maintaining the natural order of human societies. But, much more significantly, argumentation in the practical context of law (seeking agreements and adjudication), involves appealing to, not simply a shared rationality, but shared values; and it therefore requires a common conscience. In other words, if the rule of law is the absolute rule of justice, a society requires a shared definition of justice.

Prof. Hoppe, at the 2017 meeting of the Property and Freedom Society, puts essentially the same argument thus: 'Multiculturalism — cultural heterogeneity — cannot exist in one and the same place and territory without leading to diminishing social trust, increased tension and ultimately the call for a strongman and the destruction of anything resembling a libertarian social order.'

In medieval Europe, the Church was able to develop the world's first proper *system* of law out of the sometimes conflicting, privately developed laws prior — common, customary and Roman etc. This followed the Papal Revolution, when the Church established self-governance for herself and so secured the independent jurisdictions of other small communities, such as universities, setting a solid example for decentralised rulership throughout Europe. Interestingly, the Church also produced the foundations of international law which we still rely on to give order

---

9   See my article (supra), 'Estopping State Systems of Government'.

to the anarchy existing between sovereign nation states. But, most importantly, it is the shared morality which spanned Christendom that enabled folks from various kingdoms to expect similar judgments on disputes wherever they travelled, through the multiplicity of jurisdictions.

Nevertheless, all this talk of groups, communities and of widespread, shared morality strikes a nerve with many libertarians, especially Randians. But, as we have seen, it is these hyper-individualistic tendencies which cause modern libertarianism to recoil at Jeff Deist's idealisation of the family, churches and Hoppean communities, declaring these to be 'collectivist'. Perhaps it is the same mentality which thinks of law as a mere set of contracts made between two individuals with separate and perhaps wildly different moral beliefs.

Personalism — Neither Individualism nor Collectivism

So, we come full circle — there is a natural order which emerges in human societies and a natural law which would preserve that order. Experts can identify the equitable uses of violence in those societies, prudently seeking to balance our *individual aims* with *group expectations*. Such judgments assume an order comprised of *persons among persons*. For instance, as Hoppe put it, 'Alone on his island, Robinson Crusoe can do whatever he pleases. For him, the question concerning rules of orderly human conduct — social cooperation — simply does not arise. Naturally, this question can only arise once a second person, Friday, arrives on the island.'[10] When we speak of law, then, we don't simply mean the rules set by either Crusoe or Friday but those arrived at through argumentation — what we would call the conscientiousness of the group; the purpose of an independent third party is to secure this process for the parties involved.

What modern libertarianism assumes is that the market will decide

---

10 Hoppe, H. (2004). 'The Ethics and Economics of Private Property'; https://mises.org/library/ethics-and-economics-private-property (27/10/2017).

which legal system works best; however, this assumes that there is no market for injustice. I'm reminded of *The Simpsons*, when Bart tells the mob boss, Fat Tony, that crime doesn't pay; Fat Tony muses on his words as he leaves court in a convoy of limousines. But, as libertarianism embraces the idea, expressed by Deist, that 'family has always been the first line of defense against the state,' they will surely also recognise the role of the Church in creating an environment which fostered a propensity towards justice and so restrained the rise of the state. The argument is quite compelling when we consider that it was the lessening role of the Church and a growing culture of *subjective* judgment in all matters which birthed the modern state.

The sort of individualism in question is peculiar to the *modern* West, derived from the Protestant Reformation and the doctrine of *sola scriptura*, through which (generally speaking) each Christian was expected to come to their own conclusions regarding the teachings of the Bible. The once common conscience was to be privatised. The Church previously safeguarded traditions, values and institutions, such as natural law, from subjective, idiosyncratic distortions and prejudices, skilful jawboning and demagoguery; and it did so through the juristic process of argumentation. But, in the sixteenth century, Machiavelli's *Prince* taught that the Church sapped civic vitality from the masses and that the moralising of the Church kept monarchs from doing their job properly. As though monarchs had not already monopolised so much of the law for revenue purposes (becoming proto-states themselves), that the one institution which kept them from declaring superior rights (even whilst preaching their obligations to their people) would have to shrink.

The rejection of the natural law/order, during the so-called Enlightenment, led many to reassess how to temper man's brutish nature. For example, Hobbes, having declared that men are perpetually at war, concluded that a Leviathan state was required to create an artificial order. Compare this with the Medieval concept of the *negotium pacis et fides*, i.e. the interpersonal business of maintaining the peace and faith of Christendom.'[11]

---

11 See Jones, A.W. (2017) *Before Church and State: A Study of Social Order in the Sacramental Kingdom of St. Louis IX*, Emmaus Academic.

Following the Reformation, a more contractarian approach was required to maintain certainty in the law; constitutions, even Hobbes' social contract theory, became a matter of necessity for the rising modern state, which was now free to centralise all previously free institutions and instruments — churches, currencies etc. Of course, classical liberals such as Locke imbibed this fundamentally statist thinking. In practice, therefore, states now had the freedom to, as it were, make up their own rules; and so arose legal positivism.

As the legislating powers of the state have grown, especially in the last century, as well as the demand for the role of the state as a middleman for every conceivable interaction between citizens, responsibility has shifted away from the family, the community and the Church to some central coercive authority with limited liability. We might say, rather, that irresponsibility has swept our civilisation, socially mobilised from top to bottom. In our atomistic/hyper-individualistic Western societies, in which we hardly know our neighbours, the only thing which still binds us is contracts enforced by a coercive and no less self-interested body. With this unnatural system guiding our relationships, where is the incentive for a good reputation in your local community, for heartfelt, voluntary charity, for keeping a family together when times are tough etc. etc.? Across the social scale, there is only the incentive to be as litigious as is profitable, and to cover your arse against the same.

To conclude, then, if libertarians are prepared to accept the importance of communities of families as the first line of defence against the state, they should accept both the past and future role of the Church as the army fighting for ever more decentralised authority and natural law (including private property rights), and against the monopolisation of judicial services. This is more than simply accepting more traditionalist ideas, perhaps because one feels more comfortable with conservative values or some such. As Maslow's hierarchy of needs shows, people have social needs, involving belonging to a community with common values and a shared sense of transcendence; if we are to start accepting the existence of these needs, we have to be consistent and rediscover pre-modern libertarian thought as espoused by great thinkers, such as Erik von Kuehnelt-Leddihn and Prof. Frank van Dun. We may discover our footing is much stronger on *this* rock.

CHAPTER 5

Libertarianism Needs Nationalism (Not Statism)

(Why It Pays to Have a National Identity)

THE REASON MULTICULTURALISM MAKES MY blood boil is, whilst I am a libertarian, I am also strongly nationalistic. Many libertarians confuse nationalism with collectivism, statism, and racism, the implication being that if you have any sentiment for your people-group, you're no libertarian. They assume you are delusionally taking personal pride in the historical achievements of long-dead, successful European people. That is, you forget your individualistic self and imagine a racial collective which can take credit for the achievements of others who share certain genes. But that's not why I'm nationalistic at all.

Of course, I am proud of Western civilization for developing modern capitalism and an overwhelming number of other great innovations, just as I am proud of the association I have with my beautiful, bright daughter or the successes of a close friend. These things are a social benefit, however remote, to me, and so I feel a natural desire to celebrate them. However, my nationalism is based purely on my subjective values, derived from simple, socio-biological facts; not some superficial notion of 'white pride' — you know, Aristotle and Mozart were white etc.

First, nationality does not necessarily refer to the legal citizenship of a nation-state.

Eminent libertarian scholar, Murray Rothbard, noted, 'Contemporary libertarians often assume, mistakenly, that individuals are bound to each other only by the nexus of market exchange.' Therefore, any talk of groupings, such as nations, is considered as collectivist as statism. 'They forget that everyone is necessarily born into a family, a language, and a culture. Every person is born into one or several overlapping communities, usually including an ethnic group, with specific values, cultures, religious beliefs, and traditions.'[1] This is the original meaning of nation — effectively, the extended tribe.

So, why do I favour homogeneity among European-origin groups? Simply, there probably wouldn't be a libertarianism without it. One proposed socio-biological characteristic which gave rise to libertarianism in the West is high-trust society. Studies show that the societies with the highest levels of trust are characterised primarily by ethnic homogeneity, such as Japan, but especially the Nordic countries.[2] Entire empires have fallen because of the ethno-nepotistic desire to look after one's own. The Ottomans stole millions of European children from our shores for centuries in order to indoctrinate them and create Janissaries — an administrative class with no biological ties to any group apart from the state. For the same reason, the Romans posted their infantry to far-flung parts of the Empire, removing all regional ties.

As Nima Sanandaji explains in his book, *Scandinavian Unexceptionalism*, pre-existing cultural (particularly Christian) norms are responsible for the low levels of poverty among Scandinavians, both within and without Nordic countries, before and during the harmful socialistic policies adopted since the 60s and 70s. Of course, a higher average IQ, a propensity to hard work and a cultural respect for private property rights are important, but you need trustworthiness for healthy, regular trade. Without a high trust society, you won't have a significant development of trade

---

[1] Rothbard, M. (ed. 2014). 'A Libertarian View of Nationalism, Secession, and Ethnic Enclaves'; https://mises.org/blog/libertarian-view-nationalism-secession-and-ethnic-enclaves (29/10/2017).

[2] See Salter, F. (2001). *Risky Transactions: Trust, Kinship and Ethnicity*, Berghahn Books.

and prosperity; without that, you can kiss the manifestation of libertarian institutions good-bye. In short, if you love freedom, you've got to love homogeneity.

What makes this talk of national groups individualistic?

Just because Westerners organise into societies with distinct cultures, doesn't mean those cultures are collectivist, like those of East Asia. I subjectively value libertarian society, for myself and for my loved ones; the more libertarian — the freer the people — the better. I therefore value those groups which most manifest libertarian cultures and principles, and Western civilization alone has done so. The incentive, then, for my white nationalistic streak is the libertarianism of largely homogeneous European societies. Simply put, if libertarianism is to become more than an intellectual theory of law, if it is to manifest and grow in the future, it must become nationalistic.

Chapter 6

Folk-Right Versus Multiculturalism

To most Westerners today, the words 'nation', 'nationality' and 'law' seem only to mean the state, citizenship and legislation enacted by the state. But there are other meanings to these words, which were their primary and even sole meanings in the past. The nation was once the ethnic group, the tribe at large — nationality being one's ethnicity. Likewise, in Europe the law once meant the customs of the kin-group. So how is it that kinship is not only ignored by Western states as the criterion for citizenship but is even unheard of to most? And is there a future for the original understanding of these words?

Historically, nations (in the truest sense of the word) decided personhood and rights-exercising ability based on their being a member of the kin group, not according to whomever the state decided was welcome to citizenship of that nation. Prof. Ricardo Duchesne rightly points out that even the rise of Western nation-states, including the US, was not based on civic nationalism, noting their 'White-only' immigration policies. He writes,

> The nations of Europe were not mere 'inventions' or functional requirements of modernity, but were factually rooted in the past, in common myths of descent, a shared history, and a distinctive cultural tradition. While the rise of modern industry and modern bureaucracies allowed for the materialization of nation states in Europe, these nations were primordially based on a population with a collective sense of kinship.[1]

---

1 Duchesne, R. (2015). 'The Greek-Roman Invention of Civic Identity versus the Current Demotion of European Ethnicity', *The Occidental Quarterly*, 15.

Aliens have always been granted special rules—notably, being treated according to the law of their own people; this wasn't because they had the wrong passport, but because they were simply not of one's nation. Many today will presume that this was just ancient tribalism, fuelled by irrational xenophobia. However, as Prof. Duchesne notes elsewhere, the modern liberal democracy of the West denies the biological impulse to protect one's own and mistakenly assumes that this denial and even the individualistic, libertarian ideals of the West, are shared by all the peoples of the world:

> Humans are social animals with a natural impulse to identify themselves collectively in terms of ethnic, cultural and racial markers. But today Europeans have wrongly attributed their unique inclination for states with liberal constitutions to non-Europeans. They have forgotten that liberal states were created by a particular people with a particular individualist heritage, beliefs, and religious orientations... They don't want to admit openly that all liberal states were created violently by a people with a sense of peoplehood laying sovereign rights over an exclusive territory against other people competing for the same territory. They don't want to admit that the members of the competing outgroups are potential enemies rather than abstract individuals seeking a universal state that guarantees happiness and security for all regardless of racial and religious identity.[2]

This liberal ignorance of racial impulses only really became institutionalised in the 1960s, with the rise of cultural Marxism. Of course, it became more fashionable to distance oneself from ethnic and racial discrimination as this became increasingly associated with the defeated nations of World War II (as though they were the only ones with such considerations). But, as with much of classical liberalism, the basis of this anti-racialism was inspired by the same hyper-individualism which grew out of the Enlightenment and has since reduced Westerners to mere economic units, void of any meaningful cultural identity.

---

2   Duchesne, R. (2017). 'Carl Schmitt Is Right: Liberal Nations Have Open Borders Because They Have No Concept of the Political', *The Occidental Quarterly*, 17, 35–45.

With the demonisation of those who sincerely take racial and other socio-biological considerations of social order into account, Western nations were primed to accept universalistic and civic notions of citizenship.

Right of Blood

The law of citizenship around the world is based on the two Greco-Roman legal concepts—*jus sanguinis* (right of blood) and *jus soli* (right of soil). The latter grants citizenship if one is born within the national territory, as is presently the practice in the U.S. (birthright citizenship). Typically, the right of blood, that is, citizenship granted to children of citizens, is not really a radical alternative, as this most commonly goes hand-in-hand with *jus soli*.

The Constitution of Liberia, which limits citizenship to 'persons who are Negroes or of Negro descent', and the original United States Naturalization Law, which limited naturalization to immigrants who were 'free white persons of good character', are examples of *jus sanguinis*. However, most Western nations have adopted the 'proposition nation' idea of civic nationalism in which citizenship is only a matter of accepting principles like democracy and constitutional government. Only a few decades ago, the term 'British' still had a primarily ethnic meaning but, today, the civic meaning is dominant by far.

This is an unsustainable mistake which leaves the ethnic groups of Europeans vulnerable to those aliens who are conscious of their ethnic loyalties and are willing to take advantage of a democratic system which pits all conceivable groups against each other in competition to wield political power. We cannot ignore the fact of ethnic nepotism—we are all, as individuals, in competition with others over resources in order to achieve our aims, whatever they may be. Moreover, stoked by the identity politics of the left, group membership continues to function as an important source of identity. Competition therefore becomes between-group competition which whites will lose in the long run as the demographic tide turns against them.

The concept I propose, that of folk rights, takes these matters into account to identify the natural order. To achieve it, we must begin by repealing birthright citizenship and thus re-institutionalise the right of blood. How can this be justified?

Biology draws a line within which it is rational to extend our altruism. Ordinarily, we only make significant sacrifices for our immediate family; what sort of parents wouldn't put their child's interests before those of another? But Frank Salter, in *On Genetic Interests: Family, Ethnicity, and Humanity in an Age of Mass Migration*, argues that groups who share a greater percentage of their genes form 'ethnies' — biological populations which will act for the welfare of the group in times of need. Thus, when endangered, individuals extend their protective impulses to the ethny (ethnic kinship), as a natural extension of familial kinship.

Biology therefore sets natural boundaries around whom we are prepared to extend our individual recognition of kinship to. This not only makes the ethny the most practical focus of self-interest, but it also explains why human societies have near-universally done so as matter of intuition. Members of our ethnic/racial in-group should be seen as family, albeit less related than biological families, but definitely far more closely related than people from different races. Naturally, such interests are best protected with laws of *jus sanguinis*.

Those who point to vague boundaries between groups should recognise that our nations have been largely ethnically homogeneous throughout their history, until the very recent onslaught of non-white immigration into European-dominated areas. Population genetic research has conclusively shown genetic discontinuities between the major human races.[3] The Japanese, as one of many other examples, do not have a problem identifying their own.

As a strongly libertarian lover of Western civilization, to which such individualism is unique, I believe it is important that the natural, socio-biological order of the European civilizations be maintained. It is indeed

---

3   See Cochran, G. & Harpending, H. (2015). *10,000 Year Explosion: How Civilization Accelerated Human Evolution*, Basic Books; or Wade, N. (2015). *A Troublesome Inheritance*, New York: Penguin Books.

in our self-interest to do so, but self-interest is the prime law of nature, and the individualism so loved by libertarians could soon be a distant memory as our societies are increasingly dominated by groups that are not so inclined at all. Living now in the post-migration, multi-racial West, composed of competing groups defined on the basis of ethnicity, we must realise that our legitimate self-interest aligns with furthering the interests of our racial group and European civilization.

Part Two
SOCIO-BIOLOGY

CHAPTER 1

In Search of Non-White Philosophers

PHILOSOPHY STUDENTS FROM SOAS (SCHOOL of Oriental and African Studies) University of London, have demanded their syllabus comprise a majority of Asian and African philosophers. In an attempt to 'address the structural and epistemological legacy of colonialism', they have shown themselves to be completely ignorant of the history and indeed the nature of philosophy itself.[1] As Sir Roger Scruton rightly put it, 'If they think there is a colonial context from which Kant's *Critique of Pure Reason* arose, I would like to hear it.'[2] Nevertheless, I don't even think one can study a legitimate philosophy course with a minority of white philosophers in the course material. A mere glance at non-white philosophy is enough to prove my point. The post-colonial world of African philosophy is simply reactionary and ethnocentric and so, as a school, hasn't contributed anything new or substantial to the body of philosophy *in toto*. Well then, what about the pre-colonial world, going back to ancient times?

---

1 See an article from *The Independent* here: http://www.independent.co.uk/news/uk/home-news/soas-university-of-london-students-union-white-philosophers-curriculum-syllabus-a7515716.html (27/10/2017).

2 From the *Mail on Sunday*, issue 08/01/2017; http://www.dailymail.co.uk/news/article-4098332/They-Kant-PC-students-demand-white-philosophers-including-Plato-Descartes-dropped-university-syllabus.html (27/10/2017).

Surely, Africans have contributed enough to warrant at least a semester?

Of course, the Egyptians! They lived on the African continent and so, logically, we must conclude that their nobles and kings were all black. Not at all. Tutankhamun's mummy has well-preserved fair hair and facial features, as do his grandparents, and he has Western European DNA — just one example, supported by other archaeological evidence besides.[3] The Pharaohs were white until around 800 B.C. and again later, when Ptolemy ruled Egypt in Alexander's wake, making Cleopatra et al. white too.

Yet, many will still insist that we don't know this for sure, and will dismiss the evidence with accusations of 'scientific racism'. More than this, however, many black youths embarrassingly assert the much-derided statement, 'We were kings!' due to the deliberate ambiguity introduced by leftist academia. There is no evidence that the great thinkers of Egypt were black; rather the opposite is true.

But St. Augustine of Hippo was African; he states he is African in his writings, doesn't he?

Augustine was African, yes, but he was undoubtedly a Caucasian. His mother was a Berber and his father, Patricius, was of the upper-class and could not have held that name or that position if he was anything other than a white man. Kings, blacks have been — but major Christian philosophers? No.

So then we're left with Yoruba and Bantu — the former, a primitive form of spiritism; the latter, another religion with a belief in a supreme

---

3   See Reuters article 'Half of European men share King Tut's DNA'; https://uk.reuters.com/article/oukoe-uk-britain-tutankhamun-dna/half-of-european-men-share-king-tuts-dna-idUKTRE7704OR20110801 (27/10/2017).

being, the philosophy of which views beings and forces as synonymous or at least thinks primarily in terms of the forces which bring things into existence. But this is hardly something overlooked by all of the various competing schools of thought in Western philosophy.

Let's move into Asia for our course material, then.

The Islamic world produced some great thinkers; surely we can get some great non-white thinkers from here? Alas, no. If it's white philosophers you want, you've come to the right place. The Persians were Indo-Aryan peoples — kinsmen of the nomadic white people who migrated West into Europe — but who chose to travel South-East instead. Yes, Zoroastrianism was developed by white people. Furthermore, the greatest Islamic philosophy was produced by brilliant Iranians, *despite* Islam, and their work was based heavily on Plato and Aristotle — yet more white men.

Many have recently complained that the upcoming biopic of Rumi, the 13th century Sufi mystic, should not star Leonardo DiCaprio as the poet, because Rumi wasn't white. But, as Jason Reza Jorjani explains, 'When [Rumi] was born in 1207, Khorasan was still ethnically white.'[4] Khorasan was a hotbed for esoteric interpretations of the Qur'an, being a former strongly Zoroastrian area which produced a large number of important Persian scientists and poets.

Well, what about the Chinese?

Just as today, Asian governments seek to remedy their so-called creativity deficit, so too in history, the East Asian people have been superior at assimilating received knowledge, but not innovating new concepts. So, whilst I find classical Taoism quite beautiful, it is apparent that the Chinese made no distinction between the sacred and profane in their philosophy and so they simply accepted whatever was written by some previous

---

4   Jorjani, J. R. (2016). 'Rumi Was White'.

sage, and only ever concerned themselves with adaptation or preservation. Duchesne notes the contrast with the West in *The Uniqueness of Western Civilization*:

> The West, I believe, has always embodied a reflective sense of self-doubt about what it knows and what remains to be known, a kind of restlessness that has been both destructive and productive of new literary styles, musical trends, visual motifs, and novel ideas. By contrast, the intellectual and artistic order of China has remained relatively stable throughout its history.[5]

Truly, philosophy is the creation of the restlessly rationalising mind of Western man, a unique trait of our civilisation, as noted by many scholars. We alone have welcomed competing schools of thought, such has been the Western hunger for knowledge of the unknown, both inner and outer.

So, there can be no philosophy course without much-maligned, dispossessed and disenfranchised white men. This sort of racism, foisted upon us by fellow white people no less than any other group, must cease. Thankfully, in the study of those faculties largely developed by white men, the natural limits of this racism are manifest. Truly, in European civilisation alone, philosophy lives, moves and has its being. If you want a course on mysticism and primitive religions, the world is your oyster. But if you want a philosophy course with no white philosophers, you have a better chance of finding a course about rap music with no black people or a course about Kung Fu with no Asians, because at least there *are* significant white figures in those fields. All this may sound harsh, but sometimes naughty teenagers, like the SOAS student union, need to be spanked to remind them they still have some growing up to do.

---

5   Duchesne, R. (2011). *The Uniqueness of Western Civilization*, Leiden: Brill, p. 194.

Chapter 2

Why There Are No Successful Black Nations... Yet!

There is an assumption I would like you to make: I am white and not racist.

Who am I kidding? I'm writing about Africa in biological and economic terms. How dare I impose myself? Haven't white people done enough damage?

Actually, that's precisely what I contest: I don't think we've done anywhere near enough damage to warrant blaming white and Arab slavers for 'the painful fact that most African and Caribbean nations have either failed or are about to collapse'. This quote comes from a *Foreign Policy* magazine article by Prof. Chigozie Obioma, titled 'There Are No Successful Black Nations'. Rather, I think that blaming white people prevents blacks from finding the right solution.

Prof. Obioma notes that there is no country in the world 'where the black man is dignified.'

In the same breath, almost as a knee-jerk reaction, he wants to pass blame: 'History dealt us an unforgiving blow in the incursion of foreigners into black lands', referring to Arab and European enslavement and colonisation. But, this immediately begs the question: why have similar acts not had a similar effect on ethnically disparate nations?

Nigerians are very dear to me because of their glorious sense of humour and their relatively strong middle class, which have accumulated enough capital to educate their children in the West. But even Nigeria, 'the most populous black nation on Earth, is on the brink of collapse.' Prof. Obioma comes very close to ceasing all lament about blacks' problems and looking for their cause *within* their own populations rather than blaming some other group:

> *'As long as we continue to ignore our own self-assessment…we will remain the undignified race.'*

Prof. Obioma undertakes the task; so, what is the main symptom in need of resolution? He writes, 'If we, black people everywhere, cannot gather the resources within our powers to exert real changes and restore our dignity, we will continue to be seen as weak.' He makes an excellent point, but a major obstacle to this goal is that Africans haven't undergone the sort of environmental and cultural changes that Asians and especially Europeans have for thousands of years — agriculture, advanced trading cities, saving for winter etc. etc. The civic environments which developed on other continents radically altered the state of play for natural selection. Even bigger was the impact of many centuries of Christendom.

Africans, whilst having sadly lost many connections to their ancient tribal ancestry, have more importantly not had the time or the environment to develop the work ethic, familial values and natural desire to delay gratification. Thus, Ghana and South Korea, which were at similar levels of development in the 1960s, are completely different today; South Korea is a first-world nation state but Ghana hasn't much improved.

What's more, the West has spent trillions trying to improve the economy of African countries.

Therefore, it is not necessarily that most black people *cannot* gather resources, but rather that so many do not want to accumulate capital over a long period. In economics this is called time preference — the ability to put off gratification is low time preference and, conversely, blowing your monthly wage on booze and cigarettes is high time preference. How else could East Asians have taken so successfully to industrial, modern capitalism, if not because they have a strong middle class with certain values and natural tendencies?

It is foolish to ignore genes and culture when, for example, considering why blacks are disproportionately represented in violent crime wherever they are found in the world, and East Asians, the exact opposite. Blaming white people for this may be good for guilt-tripping more welfare but, as Prof. Obioma notes, this 'does nothing to inspire respect' and only encourages dependency. But, the very act of moaning about the white man and denying any personal responsibility for the failure of black communities and countries the world over, despite their receiving lots of money from the white man, is *also* a sign of weakness, and does nothing to inspire confidence.

After all, the Barbary Slave Trade saw whites being enslaved by pirates from North Africa between the 16th and 18th century. Why do Europeans not frequently complain that the Ottomans stole many more children from our shores to be forced into slavery than whites ever did from African shores? Why are some Asian clans not demanding reparations from their once conquering neighbours? We can take care of ourselves, that's why.

I propose that African-origin peoples focus on developing stronger Christian middle classes. Black countries will probably never meet the cultural and economic expectations of the West. But, as they develop in their own way, there are important lessons they can learn from Western history.

Obviously, many will complain that these socio-biological factors, which contributed to the development of First World countries, are insurmountable in the short-term — and right they are! But Christianity is perhaps the best cultural technology for incentivising those behavioural changes which result in powerful epigenetic effects in the short-term, as well as the most sustainable values for sexual selection in marriage for the long-term. Black majority countries should look to Western history and recognise that Christianity mitigated the Dark Age, following the disappearance of Western Rome, and built the greatest civilisation the world has ever known against fearsome odds.

So, what are the short-term and long-term social benefits of Christianity?

In *Biohistory: Decline and Fall of the West*, Jim Penman argues that all civilisations move in epigenetic cycles, fuelled by environmental factors such as famine, religion and war, which change the temperament of a nation. He claims that Christianity produced social changes, particularly through familial behaviour, i.e. the way children were raised and women were treated. Previously children had been largely ignored or beaten; the Church encouraged them to be schooled and nurtured. Penman claims these changes helped produce the great revolutions in European history, by reducing stress levels and increasing positive psychological developments. Other important factors were the promotion of chastity and the nuclear family.

Obviously, the dissuasion of anti-social behaviour is very valuable also for developing healthy trading relationships. In computer simulations of the famous prisoner's dilemma scenario, through numerous iterations of interactions between individuals with different temperaments, it has been found that cheaters only prosper if a very small number of interactions occur. But, in the real-life world of business, repeat interactions over many years are the norm. So, what is more beneficial for the long game?

'Blessed *are* the meek: for they shall inherit the earth', said Christ. Exactly right! The 'tit-for-tat' strategy always dominates over cheaters in the long run and creates a far more cooperative environment for trade. No wonder we humans, the most successful species on the planet, are so social. But even better is the strategy 'tit-for-tat *with forgiveness*'. These units would randomly forgive others who had cheated them previously. This is so significant in the simulations because it avoids the possibility of getting trapped into long cycles of retaliation; consider the cliché blood feud. The firm, fair but forgiving units end up dominating the simulation every time. Consider then the wonders this could do for African trade; after all, as Christianity and its work ethic grows in China, so too does the Chinese economy.

But the socio-biological benefits of Christianity do not end there. For example, in promoting chastity, among other ideal virtues, the Church encourages careful selection when choosing a spouse, producing much more sustainable family units in which to nurture those important values for the future economy of black nations. Not least among those values are of course the cardinal virtues of prudence and temperance, and the consequent eschewing of greediness and other impatient, high-time-preference behaviours; in time, this could lead to less corruption and an infrastructure of real economic growth.

However, so long as blacks pander to leftist ideals for welfare's sake, they will not only help to destroy the economies of those Western countries they live in, but also any hope of developing their own in majority black countries. After all, if they want at least one majority black nation to stand on its own two feet with dignity, what advice would leftists offer? As Prof. Walter Block joked, 'Why are we giving poor countries foreign aid? Just tell them to raise their minimum wage!'

If we Westerners want to help, we could afford to trade more directly with business-owners in African countries. Trusting that government-aid, sent to some despot, will find its way to those seeking to build businesses is folly. Also, trusting that the removal of said despot will radically alter the political situation of said countries is equally foolish. As Ilana Mercer, author of *Into the Cannibal's Pot: Lessons for America from Post-Apartheid South Africa*, noted, 'Surely by now it should be common knowledge that in Africa, you replace a despot, but not despotism; you oust a tyrant, but not tyranny?'

To conclude, it is no coincidence that those individuals with higher

IQs tend to be more economically successful and, naturally, countries with higher average IQs are too. But, if black nations wish to up their game, they should heed the advice of Penman and learn from the West's successes *and mistakes*. Whilst Prof. Obioma and others cannot find the help they need from leftist ideology, which compels them to promote socially and economically degenerative policies, they can find it from those who care enough to tell the truth, though they are called 'racist'. In an interview with Penman, I asked him which countries could expect to see the biggest improvements in the next century; he was sure that, if Christianity continued to grow, some would be African.

CHAPTER 3

Why Libertarianism Is Unique to 'the West'

MOST DENY THAT GENETICS AND cultural developments have anything to do with the success of the West. Environmental determinism as exemplified by Jared Diamond, author of *Guns, Germs, and Steel*, explains everything in terms of environmental influences rather than an interplay of genes, culture and environment—what Greg Cochran and the late Henry Harpending called the 'endless dance of biological and cultural change' in their brilliant book, *The 10,000 Year Explosion*.

Popular historian Prof. Niall Ferguson is famous for presenting six 'killer apps' which set 'the West apart from the rest'. But these are presented as tick-boxes to be imposed by some state; as though, overnight, any population could suddenly become identical to white middle-class people in the West. After all, that's what happened in Iraq, right? No. **Saying that competition, science, property, modern medicine, consumerism and a strong work ethic made Westerners more successful is putting the cart before the horse. Culture is a manifestation of the individuals interacting within a society.** It is a bottom-up, organic process; the success of the West wasn't something created by the state but by individual Westerners *despite* the rise of statism. Yet, there is still tremendous, even legislated resistance, to accepting any role whatsoever that biology may have played in the successes of any group of people.

To understand why, I spoke with Richard Lynn, Professor Emeritus of Psychology at the University of Ulster. **'Political correctness is the root of the explanation of this problem,'** Lynn told me. 'People differ genetically and if you say, for example, that some people are more intelligent than others, this is going to hurt the feelings of the less intelligent. This is the reason there is such resistance to accepting the truth.'

Not wanting to hurt any 'feelings' has not only caused academic institutions to provide their students safe-spaces to shelter them from the real world; they've been safe-spacing *all* of us from the facts. For example, **it is now in vogue to deny the existence of different races (not just genders), and to dismiss IQ as a strong indicator of future success.** In fact, it is a career-killer to discuss genes as determining almost anything — except for homosexuality of course. Just ask Helmuth Nyborg, former Professor of Psychology at Aarhus University in Denmark. He lost his job (but was cleared of misconduct allegations) for daring to investigate why the average IQ in Europe is lowered by accepting large numbers of immigrants from the Third World; thus, prompting popular scientist, Prof. Steve Pinker, to note, 'No one has the right to legislate the truth.' So, to hell with political correctness; I want the truth!

What Makes Europeans Different?

First, Prof. Lynn explained that you can distinguish Europeans as a race. That's right, races exist! In the past, the perceived races were the big three — mongoloids, negroids and caucasoids. But, as ethnicities or subgroups develop greater differences, they form definite race groups. Prof. Lynn says that we can distinguish as many as ten races, depending on how we define the clusters of gene variations — Native Americans, Arctic peoples, Europeans, Sub-Saharan Africans, Bushmen, North Africans and South Asians, East Asians, South-East Asians, Pacific Islanders and Aboriginal Australians.

Environment only explains how certain biological qualities could have evolved, but not what they are. It has been hypothesised that European libertarian and individualistic cultures and institutions are **the result of four socio-biological qualities: IQ, time preference, testosterone, and psychopathy.** It so happens that ethnic Europeans fall between the East

Asians (China, Korea and Japan) at the higher end of the spectrum, and the Bushmen and Aboriginal Australians at the other (but closer to the East Asians) on all these factors. For example, for the average East Asian IQ is 110, for Europeans it is 100 and Bushmen average at just over 60. Having a relatively high IQ with moderate levels of testosterone and psychopathy has culminated in a general spirit which was described by Spengler as 'Faustian' in its restlessness.

So, to rival Prof. Ferguson's 'killer apps' of the West, I shall present my own in the helpful acronym, **W.E.S.T.**:

Wits

Higher IQs in Northern climes are relatively easy to explain, Prof. Lynn insisted. Humans had to adapt to survive colder environments. In order to build fires, make clothing and think ahead (i.e. winter is coming), one had to be smart and also possess a low time preference. Every winter weeded out the less intelligent from the gene pool. Prof. Lynn's Cold Winters Theory of the development of higher IQ has become widely accepted.

Similarly, Gregory Clark's widely accepted theory in *A Farewell to Alms* is that the Anglo-Dutch economic miracle, which has been making the world an increasingly fun place to live for the past 300 years, was a result of our middle classes out-breeding the lower since the Late Middle Ages. What's more, lower classes were routinely wiped out by plagues and diseases, meaning that downward social mobility replaced them with the survivors from higher classes, raising the overall IQ, work ethic and sense of familial responsibility.

Ethos

At this point one may ask himself, '**But what makes the West so different from the advanced East Asian civilisations? After all, they have higher IQs than Western nations and Japan, in particular, has a high trust society.**'

Thousands of years ago, China was developing great states with a single despotic leader who subdued the population and exterminated non-conformists. Meanwhile, something completely different was happening in Europe. As Prof. Ricardo Duchesne shows in his magnum opus, *The Uniqueness of Western Civilization*, Europeans and the unique societies we produce are descended from the Indo-Europeans. These were warrior nomads from the Pontic-Caspian Steppe who evolved to value kudos from peers above their very own lives. This didn't merely produce berserker warfare and the heroic sagas of both Northern and Southern Europe, but also **libertarian aristocracies.** They were libertarian in that they did not force others to submit to their sovereign authority, as did the oriental despots, but rather sought to sincerely earn the respect of their peers.

One of the major differences between East Asians and Europeans are their respective levels of psychopathy. I have written elsewhere on Prof. Lynn's work regarding the differing levels of psychopathy in different ethnic groups.[1] Now, psychopathy does not necessarily mean antisocial, sociopathic, violent traits. Indeed, **moderate psychopathy, consisting of Factor 1 psychopathic traits, includes quite desirable qualities,** producing the most charming and charismatic characters we know — captains of enterprise, the life and soul of parties etc. With this in mind, Prof. Lynn has shown that whites have a higher average level of psychopathy than East Asians, whose ancient despotic states have long domesticated any individualistic assertiveness out of them. Yet they are moderate when compared to the higher average levels of Africans which, as Prof. Lynn has explained in his article, 'Racial and Ethnic Differences in Psychopathic Personality', lead to a higher propensity to antisocial behaviour. How then does this Faustian, moderate psychopathy manifest Western civilisation?

It has been hypothesised that the relatively higher average degree of Factor 1 psychopathic traits in Europeans, inherited from Indo-European ancestors, was as much responsible for their flouting of their own lives in berserker warfare, as it is for the characteristics of today's white man — so

---

1 See 'Source of the Faustian West' below.

restlessly curious and competitive that he must conquer all boundaries, being the first to the poles and ever outwards, even to the moon. This flagrant disregard for one's own physical safety in order to achieve immortal fame typifies Spengler's Faustian spirit.

Prof. Lynn certainly agrees that the higher degree of psychopathy in the West has historically produced a willingness to 'stick one's neck out and dissent from received opinion, like Galileo or Darwin.' This led to the West becoming more creative and dynamic, overtaking China in terms of innovation around 1500; whereas the Japanese proverb declares, 'The nail that sticks out gets hammered down!'

Since Plato, what we call 'the West' has been marked by that inner quest to plunge to the depths of the human psyche and conquer oneself, as well as one's surroundings. The competition to 'know thyself' produced philosophy, but it was the peculiarly European ethos of welcoming competitors, whose kudos one valued, which allowed its different schools of thought to exist. Whilst the Chinese sage would never have disagreed with a previous sage, Aristotle was welcome to disagree with Plato.

Thus, various political, religious and scientific revolutions are everywhere in Western history, whereas the Chinese are currently concerned about their creativity deficit, despite their brilliant ability to handle received methods and opinions. **Moderate psychopathy, therefore, seems to be the source of the individualism which has given rise to the libertarian streak of the West.** This produced an intellectually restless people, innovating the various schools of Greek philosophy and the scientific method etc. in a spirit of rational competition. Note that such movements did not and probably could not develop in the Islamic or Chinese civilisation, despite their technological advances.

Sensibility

Of course, I wanted to call this factor 'Rationalism', but that doesn't begin with S. Nevertheless, the meaning is the same — wisdom and prudence. It was Weber who pointed out the higher degree of rationalism in the

European mindset, accounting for our desire to systematise all of our enterprises. This was of course what fuelled the kind of thinking which gave birth to the numerous civilising Revolutions of Europe, not least of all the Industrial. The most unique institution of the West is Law.

Cold winters favoured those stricter adherents to the group's honour code, designed for cooperation and survival. **Even the ferocious Indo-Europeans, from whom Europeans are descended, developed libertarian aristocracies. Their legacy was the equity of free men, bound to each other in honour, oaths, and fealty.** This, in turn, affected the development of Western systems of government. Up until the Late Medieval Period and the rise of modernism and consequent statism, Western civilisation was marked by being both advanced, yet without any proper states, but there was most certainly law and order to which all were accountable, including the king. This law, however, was private — something almost inconceivable to the mindset of Western man today.

As Prof. Bruce L. Benson puts it:

> It is a widely held belief that state governments and law develop together and, therefore, that law and order could not exist in a society without the organized, authoritarian institutions of the state... [But,] law can be imposed from above by some coercive authority, such as a king, a legislature, or a supreme court, or law can develop 'from the ground' as customs and practice evolve.[2]

The process of developing a rational system of law that is *not* simply some legislation imposed by authoritarian means was a uniquely European enterprise, prompting the late Prof. S. Prakash Sinha to develop his thesis that law itself is actually a unique, non-universal institution of Western Civilisation. All of Christendom benefited from these rational systems of law.

Prof. Duchesne notes that the Church was able to maintain independent law-making ability for itself, as well as private courts across the continent,

---

2   Benson, B. L. (1990). *The Enterprise of Law: Justice Without the Law*, Pacific Research Institute for Public Policy, pp. 11–12.

producing not just the 'first comprehensive and rational systematization of law', but turning all of Europe into a 'warren of jurisdictions' with numerous sources and kinds of private law—'which in turn resulted in the preconditions and the experience for a civil society where no authority, not even the pope or the king, had complete political, religious, or intellectual jurisdiction.'[33] This stateless decentralisation would produce the very legal systems which still undergird most law around the world.

As the renowned Prof. Jonathan Haidt's almost unique study of libertarians concluded, **libertarians have 'a relatively cerebral, as opposed to emotional, cognitive style'**.[4] I have hypothesised that the greater number of Myers-Briggs 'Rationalist' personality types among whites might explain their superior, i.e. dominant, more rational and libertarian, legal systems.[5]

Temperance

The willingness to defer gratification, called 'low time preference', is crucial for advanced civilisations. Like all the above factors, this too can be partly explained by cold winters: As early humans migrated, they had to keep moving to avoid over-foraging and threats from competition. Some encountered increasingly colder environments and those who were unwilling to forgo the pleasure of consuming food immediately were unable to survive the harsher winters and thus became food for someone else.

This produced a population better able and more willing to defer gratification with each successive generation. **Lower time preference produced a culture with a superior work ethic and enabled the development of a population better able to sustain the various traits of Western civilisation,** as identified by Prof. Ferguson and others. As discussed above,

---

3   Duchesne, R. (2011). *The Uniqueness of Western Civilization*, Leiden: Brill, p. 275.

4   Iyer R., Koleva S., Graham J., Ditto P., Haidt J. (2012). 'Understanding Libertarian Morality: The Psychological Dispositions of Self-Identified Libertarians', *PLoS ONE* 7(8): e42366; https://doi.org/10.1371/journal.pone.0042366 (27/10/2017).

5   See 'Is There a European Personality Type?' below.

Europeans have their temperance to thank for those more libertarian systems of law and government which have informed so much of the West's development.

Temperance is not to be confused with timidity. Yes, cold winters, agriculture and trade favoured those who could smile and say, 'Thank you, come again,' but, whereas the East Asians have very low average levels of psychopathy and testosterone, European levels are significantly higher. Truly, we should be celebrating the social importance of our Faustian competition for self-mastery.

Nietzsche sums it up well — 'Of all evil I deem you capable: Therefore I want good from you. Verily, I have often laughed at the weaklings who thought themselves good because they had no claws.' This reminds me of John Wayne's line in *McLintock*: 'You've got to be a man first before you can be a gentleman.' However, Nietzsche complained of this competition in temperance (especially as realised by Catholic Europe) and bemoaned the introduction of it as a virtue in Ancient Greece, and the complimentary recognition of hubris as a vice. Rather, I argue that this important development was the birth of the West as a 'civilisation' and the chivalric knight or gentleman as the ideal Western man, even the ideal king.

Whereas oriental despotism legislated greater control of others, this was seen as the result of inner-weakness in the eyes of the ancient Greeks. For millennia, the Chinese lived under large centralised states which effectively domesticated their populations, resulting in the major differences identified above. It wasn't a lack of strength but rather a show of tremendous inner strength which brought about the advanced stateless societies of old Europe.

This Faustian desire to be recognised as the most composed and prudent ensured European/American libertarian systems of government and law for many centuries. It was no longer just the Indo-Europeans' competition among aristocratic peers but the added competition in temperance, among all men, which limited the king's *dominium* but not his *imperium*. That is, kings understood the long-term prudence of undertaking greater obligations for the good of their kinsmen, but not greater rights.

What's more, it was the Church which acted as that institution to ensure the rule of law (a necessary institution, as Carl Schmitt rightly identified) and encouraged kings to embody the ideal European man.

This ideal was not just for kings to manifest but for all heads of houses. The process of encouraging all men towards the aristocratic virtues was being perfected by the Church; however, as Renaissance kings sought greater irresponsibility from the social obligations expected of them, this became an easier and more lucrative model for the populace to ape, particularly the bourgeoisie and the increasingly dominant merchant and banking classes of the cities. This attitude would produce the hyper-individualistic elements of modernism and the end of personalism in Europe. Hence, one mustn't blame Christendom for the increasingly juvenile behaviour of Western man, but rather individuals who pass responsibility to an increasingly irresponsible state system of government. For such men, the short-term benefits outweigh the long.

Nietzsche was wrong about temperance, just as he was about the Church. **If we want our men to behave like men, we need them to be responsible, directly responsible for their families and the communities they form. This requires them to be strong enough to get the job done and temperate enough to make prudent long-term decisions.**

Conclusion

These 'killer apps' make Western civilisation what it is—a combination of evolutionary factors, including genes and culture, not a tick-list to be mimicked by the rest of the world. **We cannot be something we are not**, nor can we expect the rest of the world to be just like us. We wouldn't drop a Russian in the middle of the Australian desert and expect him to survive in the same way an aborigine does. Likewise, we should stop dreaming of the West making the world 'safe for democracy' or whatever else is in vogue with the political class. **Also, we must bring an end to multicultural experiments which have only resulted in the endangerment of Western civilisation.**

Prof. Haidt, has predicted that an increasingly 'diverse' society will so reduce trust as to make it unsustainable and dangerous:

> A multiethnic society is a very hard machine to assemble and get aloft into the air. ... Politics is always about factions, always about competing groups. ... But in a world in which factions are based on race or ethnicity, rather than economic interests, that's the worst possible world. It's the most intractable world we can inhabit, and it's the one that will lead to the ugliest outcome.[6]

In short, **the genocidal fascination with which immigration and diversification are imposed on the West does not spell a happy ending for any of the groups involved.** The world is more interesting when there are variety and competition, and Western civilisation has and still benefits the world greatly. If this is to continue, the above factors must be maintained — a responsibility borne by us all.

---

6 Illing, S. (2017). 'Why social media is terrible for multiethnic democracies'; https://www.vox.com/policy-and-politics/2016/11/15/13593670/donald-trump-jonathan-haidt-social-media-polarization-europe-multiculturalism.

Chapter 4

Source of the Faustian West

AFTER ACHILLES HAD DEFEATED HECTOR in battle, his chariot dragged Hector's corpse by the heels. Such was the hubristic spirit of our Indo-European ancestors — warrior nomads who conquered and ruled peoples from Europe to Asia, millennia before anyone had heard of Alexander. But the same spirit which restlessly pursued immortality in fame and glory would not only cause their European descendants to circumnavigate the globe and conquer its poles, but map the human genome also; not only has the white man needed to tower into the skies and conquer the moon, but that spirit has searched the depths of its own soul to master itself. Achilles was visited that night by Priam, King of Troy and father of Hector, who tearfully requested the burial of his son's body and reminded Achilles of his own father. Achilles called a truce for the funeral — the honour of the magnanimous gentleman, Plato's rational self-mastery, was born.

Both inwards and outwards, rationally and empirically, with brains and brawn, the spirit of the white man has continued to restlessly pursue glory, pushing whatever boundary it perceives, conceptual or physical. Like Prometheus, we would flout the gods in order to victoriously bring illumination to mankind, ever reaching into the infinite, like Faust (the Prometheus of the Renaissance) — even if it will cost us our lives, like Frankenstein (The Modern Prometheus).

> Cattle die and kinsmen die,
> thyself too soon must die,
> but one thing never, I ween, will die,
> fair fame of one who has earned.
> — *Hávamál*, 75

But what is it about Europeans that gives us this high 'tendency towards the infinite', as Spengler put it? What is the source of what he called the 'Faustian' spirit of the West?

Sadly, the study of genes as they relate to race differences is yet another dogmatic boundary the white man finds himself confronted with in our time; but I am far from the first one to vault it. We Europeans find ourselves on the scale of most IQ measurements residing above Africans, but just under the East Asians (Japan, Korea and China). So what 'x factor' has caused us to be overwhelmingly overrepresented in the number of great intellectual achievements of the past 3000 years?[1] I believe the answer lies in psychopathy.

Now, it is worth repeating that psychopathy does not necessarily mean antisocial, sociopathic and violent traits, but rather includes very desirable qualities. Whites have a higher average level of psychopathy than East Asians, whose ancient despotic states have long since domesticated much individualistic assertiveness out of them.[2] Yet we are moderate when compared to the average levels of Africans, which, as Prof. Richard Lynn has explained in his article, 'Racial and Ethnic Differences in Psychopathic Personality', leads to a higher average propensity to antisocial behaviour. This may sound mean-spirited, but my concern with the data is not to denigrate others so much as to better understand my own civilisation's place. How then has this Faustian, moderate psychopathy helped manifest Western civilisation?

In *The Uniqueness of Western Civilization*, Prof. Ricardo Duchesne has shown the origin of the Faustian spirit in the Indo-Europeans. These warlike aristocrats were only accepted as noble if they showed a willingness to sacrifice themselves in combat to achieve immortality for their name, which did not necessarily implicate any sexual conquest. Breeding for

---

1   Duchesne, R. (2013). 'Multicultural Historians: The Assault on Western Civilization and Defilement of the Historical Profession, Part I: Patrick O'Brien on the Scientific Revolution', *The Occidental Quarterly*, 13. pp. 53–72.

2   See Wade, N. (2015). *A Troublesome Inheritance*, New York: Penguin Books.

the trait of taking no thought for one's own life (to the extent that naked, berserker warfare became their most noble form of combat) produced a rather psychopathic people in the Europeans. Associated with creativity, this psychopathic competition for glory and esteem led to the evolution of men who restlessly found a way to go beyond whatever was currently considered rational or possible; they invented new concepts, abilities and technologies. So our inherited genes have played a significant role in the great dance between blood and environment we call 'culture'.

You can tell a lot about a people by the symbols they use; we don't need Jung to tell us that. The symbols used by the Indo-Europeans recurrently involved the rising sun. Just like them and the archetype of Prometheus, we restlessly reach out into void of the unknown, contrary to nature's design, to bring back some fire, to cast its light on us and bring more abundant life. Long may we continue the immortal quest, to infinity and beyond.

Chapter 5

Is There a European Personality Type?

> The European is interested in the world, he wants to know it, to make this other confronting him his own, to bring to view the genus, law, universal, thought, the inner rationality, in the particular forms of the world. As in the theoretical, so too in the practical sphere, the European mind strives to make manifest the unity between itself and the outer world. It subdues the outer world to its ends with an energy which has ensured for it the mastery of the world.
>
> — Hegel, Philosophy of Mind

I HAVE BECOME INCREASINGLY CONVINCED THAT there is something unique to the psychology of Europeans — some traits which produced the highly rationalistic and empirical way we have conducted practical and intellectual endeavours for centuries. Spengler observed that Europeans can alone be characterised as having an infinite thirst for the as yet unknown — what he called the Faustian spirit. Weber, similarly, described the white man as possessing a higher degree of rationalism, leading to the West's unique systematisation of law, religion and numerous other endeavours. But can we really identify a general personality type of the Europeans?

Of course, any scientific study of the matter is heavily stigmatised in the current age of egalitarianism. Nevertheless, we still have enough data to produce a hypothesis. Prof. Raymond Moody sought to test Carl Jung's theory of racial personality types, which he summarised thus:

While he recognized that one's psychological development is heavily influenced by the environment, Jung's extensive research and clinical experience also led him to conclude that the basic features of personality are basically genetically determined, not only for individuals but for whole races and cultures as well.

In other words, racial personality 'types' define our inborn predispositions, while culture permits or limits the ways in which those predispositions can be expressed as behaviour. Prof. Moody concluded that Jung was correct — there is 'a stronger biological basis to culture than we have heretofore recognized.'[1]

The Myers-Briggs Type Indicator (MBTI) personality test was developed from Jung's concept of typology, and it divided personalities into sixteen types. Influenced by Plato, the late Prof. David Keirsey helpfully categorised these into four temperaments; his adapted test is now one of the most widely used by employers worldwide.

The Four Temperaments:

- As Concrete Cooperators, Guardians speak mostly of their duties and responsibilities, of what they can keep an eye on and take good care of, and they're careful to obey the laws, follow the rules, and respect the rights of others.

- As Abstract Cooperators, Idealists speak mostly of what they hope for and imagine might be possible for people, and they want to act in good conscience, always trying to reach their goals without compromising their personal code of ethics.

- As Concrete Utilitarians, Artisans speak mostly about what they see

---

1 Moody, R. (1993). '12 Psychological Type and Ethnicity: How Do Ethnographic and Type Descriptions Compare?'; http://typeandculture.org/Pages/C_papers93/12MoodyHaw.pdf (27/10/2017).

right in front of them, about what they can get their hands on, and they will do whatever works, whatever gives them a quick, effective payoff, even if they have to bend the rules.

- **As Abstract Utilitarians, Rationals speak mostly of what new problems intrigue them and what new solutions they envision, and, always pragmatic, they act as efficiently as possible to achieve their objectives, ignoring arbitrary rules and conventions if need be.**

In his study, Prof. Moody examined students at the universities of Florida and Hawaii, concluding that, among Caucasians, 'There are significantly fewer STs ($p < .001$) [Guardians and Artisans] and more NTs ($p < .001$) [Rationals].' NTs are sometimes described as the 'conceptualists' — they possess a constant thirst for knowledge alongside a creative, innovative streak in the abstract and theoretical. This sounds a lot like Spengler's Faustian spirit, doesn't it? More interesting still, Prof. Keirsey originally named the Rational temperament, the Promethean — the mythological Titan, Prometheus, being the inspiration for the Renaissance character of Faust. Faustian spirit indeed!

European Temperament

Since his study, others have also found that 'Caucasians...have a preference for Intuition', that is, iNtuitive Thinking (NT).[2] So, it appears this personality type is more common among Europeans, which would explain why they have dominated rationalistic schools of thought. For example, 94% of libertarians are non-Hispanic whites,[3] and we have historically been

---

2   Herk, N. A., Schaubhut, N. A. & Thompson, R. C. (2009). 'Ethnic and Gender Differences in Best-Fit Type'; http://citeseerx.ist.psu.edu/viewdoc/download?doi=10.1.1.619.8867&rep=rep1&type=pdf (29/12/2017).

3   Cox, D., Jones, R. P. & Navarro-Rivera, J. (2013). 'In Search of Libertarians in America', PRRI; http://www.prri.org/research/2013-american-values-survey/ (29/12/2017).

more accepting of competing schools of thought, meaning that the past few millennia have seen Europeans overwhelmingly dominate the pursuit of philosophy.[4]

Whilst this subject is currently taboo in the West, as it may upset the feelings of some, the data suggest that this general personality type has its basis in our genes and would likely have been preserved or selected for by our ancient cultures. Elsewhere, I have written of the origins of this Faustian spirit in the moderate average levels of Factor 1 psychopathic traits in European peoples, inherited from our Indo-European ancestors.[5] In short, ancient Europeans welcomed competition in everything, even if, or especially if, it presented a risk of death and, thus, the possibility of achieving immortal fame for one's bravery.

This attitude was transferred to the field of philosophy, favouring minds which could conceptualise well and which were bold enough to speak out against the status quo. These socio-biological factors may in part explain the restless creativity with which the Europeans have rationally systematised all human endeavours. N.B. Prof. Keirsey's Rationals 'ignoring arbitrary rules and conventions if need be.' So, what is the significance of this? What do we do with this understanding of our general personality type as 'white people'?

We Europeans have historically and restlessly sought out solutions to the great mysteries, lasting and eternal achievements of the rational mind, even attainment of immortal glory in these discoveries. The ancient Greeks, likewise, outwitted and tangled with gods; during the Renaissance, typically European minds looked back to those ancestors, but having met their match in Christ, they also looked forward, envisioning the physically and spiritually perfect man and creating brilliant statues of this untainted archetype — something to be pursued in one's self. Their timeless gaze both looks deep into our soul and invites us to do the same, that we might know ourselves, according to the Delphic maxim. So — who are we?

---

4   See my article (supra) 'In Search of Non-White Philosophers'.

5   See the previous article, 'Source of the Faustian West'.

After centuries of plunging those depths of the soul through poetry and philosophy, and conquering the universe around us through science and economics, we find that we are the quest itself—always pursuing the archetype, and never perfect. We are both children of a creative God and stewards of all—the mechanism through which habitable order is constantly being established in the midst of chaos, a process whose microcosm is seen in the rational self-mastery of the archetypal European personality. In *this* pursuit, there certainly is an eternal weight of glory.

Conclusion

Yet, we find ourselves overwhelmed by those who resent us, even our fellow-Europeans, and who would have us believe lies about our history and destiny, i.e. that the best way we can transcend ourselves, as we are wont to do, is to deliberately see ourselves sacrificed out of existence. But this destructive ethno-masochism is no victory for our people — surrender is not typical for us. If we would transcend our individual selves, we must recognise that we are a distinct group with unique cultures, upholding unique ideals; looking back, we understand where we came from and learn from our mistakes, and looking forward, we eternally pursue our ideals. And the European personality type is by no means the least of these.

Chapter 6

Why Do Whites Choose White Guilt?

(Faustian Spirit is a double-edged sword)

YOU'VE SURELY ENCOUNTERED IT: WHITE people virtue-signalling how 'not racist' they are. Their displays of piety even go so far as copying black humorists' jokes about whites. It doesn't matter where in the West they come from; gender isn't a major factor, nor is one's positioning on the left/right paradigm of the modern, liberal political spectrum. But, this is not simply a passing, ingratiating fad of the puritans of progressivism; it is more serious than that.

Here is a quote from Noel Ignatiev of Harvard University: 'The goal of abolishing the white race is on its face so desirable that some may find it hard to believe that it could incur any opposition other than from committed white supremacists.'[1] Do you expect this man has lost his job or been punished in some way? He is celebrated in fact. Of course, he claims that he simply wishes to eradicate the *notion* of whiteness, since he chooses to believe there is no such thing as race. Apparently, he does not want to eradicate fair-skinned people.

Yet, imagine if the word 'white' had been replaced with Ignatiev's own ethnic group — 'Jewish'. Would he be so celebrated, for instance, had he claimed he wanted to aggressively 'abolish' all notions of the Jews as a

---

1   Ignatiev, N. (2008). 'One Summer Evening', *When Race Becomes Real: Black and White Writers Confront Their Personal Histories,* SIU Press, p. 296.

particular, chosen people of God? Why then is the eradication of European identity acceptable? And how readily would such a Marxist change his mind about eradicating fair-skinned people if he were given political power, and if said whites refused to relinquish said identity? I daresay the 20th century has taught us that lesson.

It should go without saying that the agendas of the political classes, across the West, have been complicit where the abandonment of the character of Western nations is concerned. The mainstream media too has played no small part in maintaining the volume of the message, damning and ostracising any voices discordant to it. But how could this have happened? It seems unthinkable that it could have happened *so easily* to any other people of the world, who would typically be far too proud to tolerate such a destructive cultural trend. What's so unique about white psychology that such a thing could occur?

My question was loaded, yes. It seems to me that the root cause is a psychological one. There is something peculiar to white folks which has resulted in too many of us kowtowing to the negative self-image in vogue; this something also results in us being so apologetic for our existence that we don't want to make a fuss about declining birth-rates and encroaching minority status in a few decades or less. Despite census data showing that whites are, by far, least likely to marry outside of their race, British adverts portray an excessive number of multiracial couples to show the world how 'down with diversity' we are.

What is going on in the mind of whitey?

Prof. Richard Dawkins' *The Selfish Gene* is an astoundingly intuitive book, displaying the gene-centred view of all life, which seems to put all social interactions into sound perspective. He identifies humans as 'survival machines — robot vehicles blindly programmed to preserve the selfish molecules known as genes.' Of course, Prof. Dawkins couldn't forgo atheistic overtones in his definition. But, what is the *moral* of his philosophy?

Let us try to teach generosity and altruism, because we are born selfish. Let us understand what our own selfish genes are up to, because we may then at least have the chance to upset their designs, something that no other species has ever aspired to do.²

To the white man, who possesses the hopelessly repetitive habit of universalising every principle he encounters, this is kryptonite! The trouble isn't that white people are not altruistic — we have the safest countries in the world (thanks in no small part to Christianity); the problem is that we believe we are *so* altruistic that we must save the world, whether it wants saving or not. White men have famously burdened themselves with ending slavery and promoting liberal values across the world, even at the cost of their own nations or empires. No, it wasn't *all* evil colonialism; whites wanted to teach the globe to read, and even had dreams of saving the eternal souls of the whole world.

How is being too nice a problem?

The problem is two-fold:

1. On average, whites possess a more psychopathic psychology which longs for recognition; and

2. The predominant personality type among whites produces a tendency to transcend social norms.

The result is: whites tend to presuppose that every single culture does or could or *should* exhibit the same levels of brilliance they perceive in themselves; and they have frequently coerced others to do so. For example, modern liberals, especially the neocons, act in the same way as past colonials by forcibly 'making the world safe for democracy.' But it isn't

---

2   Dawkins, R. (1989 ed.). *The Selfish Gene*, Oxford University Press, p. 3.

just abroad. At home, we increasingly surround ourselves with foreigners — the more alien the culture, the better — as an audience to bear witness to how piously far above the selfishness of our genes we have risen (as though other peoples actually care).

Basically, I propose that whites want to have their cake and eat it too. True, they predominantly marry those of their own racial grouping, i.e. those with whom they feel more comfortable and akin. But they are also fully aware that, by not having children, they can hypocritically claim they aren't at all interested in passing on their genes — they are far too pious to possess any natural, racial motivations. Really, they want *kudos* from their peers, and they want to return home to as comfortable and responsibility-free a domestic lifestyle possible.

Disagree? The Chinese aren't fooled. They know exactly the egoism afoot amongst liberal whites; thus the immense online popularity of the derogatory term, '*baizuo*', for white liberals. This Chinese term means a 'naive western educated person who advocates for peace and equality only to satisfy their own feeling of moral superiority. A *baizuo* only cares about topics such as immigration, minorities, LGBT and the environment; while being obsessed with political correctness to the extent that they import backwards Islamic values for the sake of multiculturalism… The Chinese see the *baizuo* as ignorant and arrogant westerners who pity the rest of the world and think they are saviours.'[3] These intuitive young Chinese have really identified this emperor's lack of clothes.

But, how did this moral consensus that whites must feel especially guilty for the past arise?

To answer that question, we need to understand the rise of cultural Marxism in the West. After the nihilism of the 1960s, this movement took off when it became apparent to leftist thinkers that earlier Marxists, such as

---

3   Qiuyan, Q. (2017). 'Chinese derogatory social media term for "white left" Western elites spreads'; http://www.globaltimes.cn/content/1047989.shtml (29/12/2017).

Gramsci and Lukács, were correct — the socialist experiments of the 20th century were failures, and if leftist ideology was to survive, Western *culture* would have to be subverted.[4] Much ink has been spent on the Frankfurt school etc. and just how the left came to dominate the media, academia and the political institutions in the West, but suffice it to say that the doctrine of dividing the haves from the have-nots didn't take hold. The real divisive factor which has caused massive rupture between every conceivable group in the West has been the doctrine of the oppressed and the oppressor.

Whites created modern capitalism, developed successful natural and hierarchical orders, and have come to dominate the world, culturally and otherwise. By completely subverting everything, and I mean everything, about European civilisation worldwide, a leftist social order could *then* rise from the ashes. But where to find an overwhelming group of 'the oppressed', if policies and the social dynamic are geared to improving every man from every walk of life? Naturally, the obstacle to the end goal is majority groups of white people and the kinds of cultures and civilisations they have historically produced, which are inhospitable to the weed of communism, even in its softer form of liberal democracy, since they do not appeal to the lowest common dominator.

Therefore, the long game has been the deconstruction and now the apparent abolition of the very identity of white people, nationally or otherwise. No pride in one's heritage, strengthening of one's people for the future or any other such heresy is permissible. Only absolute and hyper-individualism is permitted for the white man. Until he is an absolute minority, he can identify as an economic unit, and no more.

Prof. Hans-Hermann Hoppe summarises the phenomenon well:

> [Every] 'victim' group has thus been pitted against every other, and all of them have been pitted against white, heterosexual, Christian males and in particular those married and with children as the only remaining, legal-

---

4 See Duchesne, R. (2011). *The Uniqueness of Western Civilization*, Leiden: Brill; and Duchesne, R. (2017). *Faustian Man in a Multicultural Age*, London: Arktos Media Ltd.

ly un-protected group of alleged 'victimizers'... The institution of a family household with father, mother and their children that has formed the basis of Western civilization, as the freest, most industrious, ingenious and all-around accomplished civilization known to mankind, i.e., the very institution and people that has done most good in human history, has been officially stigmatized and vilified as the source of all social ills and made the most heavily disadvantaged, even persecuted group by the enemy elites' relentless policy of *divide et impera*.[5]

How can so many whites be so stupid?

Prof. Ricardo Duchesne, myself and others have written of the Faustian spirit of the European psychology—how something has evolved which has caused white people to attempt deeds which seem bizarre and pointless to most others. Just as the white man has sought to be *the first* to reach the poles, mountaintops and even the moon, so too I believe that the white man is endeavouring to be the first to show he has no care at all for his own genes.

The white man would show the world that he is so unconcerned with the will of his genetic programming that he can flout it altogether and be so transcendentally altruistic that he will put the well-being of all others before his own people until, perhaps, they have gone extinct. Sadly, this fearless quest for glory, inherited from our psychopathic Indo-European ancestors, isn't accompanied with intelligence or any long-term thinking. Our ancestors disregarded their lives and performed great deeds so as to be remembered and to win immortal fame—but they did so to be remembered by *their people*!

If we are *the first* to neglect our genetic predispositions towards our

---

5   Hoppe, H. (2017). 'Libertarianism and the Alt-Right. In Search of a Libertarian Strategy for Social Change', Speech delivered at the 12th annual meeting of the *Property and Freedom Society* in Bodrum, Turkey, on September 17, 2017; https://misesuk.org/2017/10/20/libertarianism-and-the-alt-right-hoppe-speech-2017/ (29/12/2017).

own, we will become a proverb of stupidity to the rest of the world, who will not remember us with fondness. Other peoples wish to recall the great deeds of *their* ancestors and heroes, not those of another. Once again, we whites universalise to our great undoing. But this time we will have no children to mourn our mistakes.

Part Three

POLITICS

Chapter 1

Liberal Supremacism: Today's White Man's Burden

For all their railing against the dynamically dominant civilisations of Europe, especially against imperialism, modern liberals unwittingly behave in precisely the same manner as the totalitarian villains of history they claim to oppose. The only difference is that they wish to impose a globalist, rather than a nationalist version of liberalism. In practice, this is very hyper-individualistic; they reject all traditional forms of identity by promoting a sense of white guilt among the native Europeans (for colonialism's sake) and, for immigrants, they peddle a replacement identity — consumerism with a veneer of some unappealing form of constitution or proposition-based civic nationalism. You know, 'Please adhere to "British values", if you find the time and if it's not too much bother' — that sort of thing.

> *Make no mistake, liberals are no less guilty of universalising their ideas and forcing them on the world.*

Prof. Ricardo Duchesne pointed out as much in his underappreciated book, *The Uniqueness of Western Civilization*. He identifies the behaviour of the left, especially in their desire to see everyone converted to their ideology, as driven by the same spirit which has historically caused Europeans to dominate others, for the sake of imposing their principles on them; principles, of course, which they perceive to be universally important. This is the liberal white man's burden — it has been shaping the world for decades and with tremendous urgency.

Today, our political spectrum is no more than two sides of the same coin — both left and right today are modern liberal democrats, whether socialist or neocon, and both wish to see the breakdown of all humanity into mere economic units. Fascism and Communism were defeated and now *they* are set to dominate the world stage. Their shared violent goal was recently evidenced by the near-unanimous celebrations of Donald Trump's 2017 Shayrat missile strike in Syria, despite the fact that this strike conflicted with the wishes of those who had elected Trump precisely for his anti-war campaign promises.

For all their rhetoric regarding decolonisation, the liberals have themselves attempted to colonise and proselytise the world. As most countries 'Westernise', they are really transforming into soulless wastelands of consumerism in the place of identity. Those who admire the colonialism of the Enlightenment era boast of improvements in healthcare, education and industry for the third world; today, the liberals boast of improved 'human rights' and technology to justify *their* endeavours. They sugar-coat their hypocrisy with euphemisms such as 'soft power', but this is no less the replacement of native, national, cultural, religious or, indeed, any collective identity than that of burdened white men past.

The similarities don't stop there. As foreign lands (with no real connection to the West) are ravaged by war, Merkel et al. call for third-world refugees to travel across the seas, heartlessly indifferent to how many will perish in the voyage. Those who survive will be forced to integrate into the same system that is gradually being imposed back in their countries of origin. It all sounds like the very international slavery which is bemoaned by the liberals (the same liberals who denigrate the only civilisation to put an end to the practice). All this serves to assimilate foreigners into the multicultural global community as a mere economic unit, one which knows no racial, ethnic, religious or cultural ties.

Looting too!

How could we forget about the looting? It has even become the mainstream academic opinion that the West was able to advance so far beyond even China, since the late medieval period, because of material as well as cultural looting from colonial territories. Of course, the fact that the GDP of colonial European countries was minute or that those countries which didn't engage in such activities were also successful, goes unmentioned. The liberals remain just as silent while far greater lootings occur every day, across the world, as international elites steal even from future generations through purposely installed central banks.

What about the majorities of white Europeans?

Today, to declare yourself a lover of European civilisation, let alone one who wishes to see it demographically preserved, is rank heresy. Such a suggestion leads to identity, national pride and all manner of threats to globalist liberalism. No, better to strip them and shame them with guilt and ostracism if they so much as suggest that their country is built on more than modern liberal propositions. All manner of derogatory terms are given legitimate power against such as these — 'racist', 'white supremacist', 'bigot' etc. — designed to destroy reputations, careers and essentially economically assassinate criticism.

Yet, the garden variety liberal doesn't seem to realise the hypocrisy of their own totalitarianism, imperialism and witch-hunting; such is the depth of their delusion. Prof. Duchesne asks,

> Is not the emphasis on cultural pluralism a form of universalism that requires modes of reflective reasoning (metacultural, historical, and anthropological) that are/were unavailable in other cultures and that threaten/have threatened the particular traditions and standards of diverse cultures? Can Westerners defend their liberal values by tolerating values which negate these liberal values? Should Westerners be deprived of their own particular traditions in the name of the universal promotion of pluralism and diversity?[1]

As we continue to oppose modern liberalism, we can use the identification of its totalitarianism as a means of putting it on the back-foot, demanding

---

1   Duchesne, R. (2011). *The Uniqueness of Western Civilization*, Leiden: Brill, p. 32.

that it answers for its destructive hypocrisy. Let us make our voice heard and give the political class pause for thought.

Chapter 2

The Neocon Slave Ethic

When you think of neocons, you probably think of mighty words like 'warmonger' or 'hawkish' — something which reflects their aggressive foreign policy. But don't mistake their principles for the strong foundations of Western civilisation. The neocons are not the spiritual descendants of the European warrior-explorers. Rather, they are draining all vitality from the West by promoting nonchalant producer/consumers to the middle classes and higher, and putting down the critically thinking man who is concerned with the bigger picture.

When we think of genuinely highbrow conversations about politics, we envisage the upper classes at dinner, the men retiring to the billiards room to continue. A crack den is *not* the first thing that springs to mind. The sincere desire to do more than, for instance, virtue signal how sincerely one has adopted the slave ethic of political correctness, is part of the Western 'Faustian' spirit. Of course, the conversation round the billiards table will not change the world overnight, but the host and guests are yet hungry to pursue the truth, long into the night, whether it is attained or not.

The neocon scoffs at such a scene, piously declaring themselves holier than such boors who would dare discuss politics and religion etc. This is their slave ethic: repressing the hearts and minds of the West one conversation at a time, if only that they might be clean enough to remain in the light of acceptable opinion which falls through the Overton window — regardless of where the left has moved it. Their Pharisaical piety, in the cathedral of political correctness, is indeed on a par with that of the leftists.

So, how is neo-conservatism a proper slave ethic?

Let's look at demographics. Domestically speaking, neocons follow the extreme racial blindness of popular neocons like Prof. Niall Ferguson, believing that radical ethnic changes in demography change nothing essential, so long as you have democracy and modern medicine — but, when it comes to the ethno-nepotism of Israel, no questions are allowed. Israel has developed a very sensible citizenship policy based on *jus sanguinis* to preserve the character and identity of the nation,[1] otherwise granting residency-status to Syrians in the Golan Heights etc. Good for them! But, whether it is criticism of Zionism, or high praise of Israel's policies, this conversation is another Pandora's box to the neocons.

In response to the master ethics of thinking for oneself and possessing the masculine virtue of protecting and preserving one's own people and traditions, neocons propose a subversive counter-ethic in which success is measured simply in how efficient an economic unit one is. Not just, figuratively, how much cotton they can pick, but how readily they will spend most of their wage, or even encumber themselves with debt, in order to add more fuel to the house-fire that is the modern Keynesian economy. But the reason for this counter-ethic isn't simply economic error, though many neocons would favour an economic system which props up the sort of spending (public or otherwise) they believe to be the cause of Western greatness.

Of course, a greater earning potential comes in large part from physiological strengths, like more testosterone, more imposing physical stature, attractiveness, general intelligence etc., but the weakness of the neocon is their inner-resentment of the traditional ideal of the thinking man. They denigrate those who objectively question the decline of the West as they know this will unmask them as rats racing cheerily to the precipice of the River Weser, to the Pied Piper of Hamelin's tune.

Their slave ethic is played out on a global scale in the form of the

---

1 See my article (supra) 'Folk-Right versus Multiculturalism'.

economic imperialism of the more Atlanticist Western countries. On the local scale, it is against those who would stand for cultural and/or ethnic homogeneity — the primary factor for creating a high trust society — or against those who refuse to turn a blind eye to interventionist foreign policy. Such thinking mortifies the neocon bourgeoisie who readily cry the modern equivalent of 'heretic'. Politics and religion are not on their table. Traditionalism? This is the 21st century, don't you know? No, the consumerist serf's idea of intellectual discussion is a tame book club in which faux-right talk is a cover for measuring each other's 'success', as is church or any other social occasion.

Neocons may have had a good run at disguising themselves as part of the 'right', but they cannot disguise the cowardly and subversive nature of their ideology, which thus betrays its origins, having no root in conservatism or traditionalism. Kuehnelt-Leddihn defines the true right to distinguish clearly whether an ideology aims to or away from the natural order: 'The right has to be identified with personal freedom, with the absence of utopian visions whose realisation — even if it were possible — would need tremendous collective efforts; it stands for free, organically grown forms of life. And this in turn implies a respect for tradition.'[2]

Being, therefore, built on sand, neo-conservatism's days are surely numbered; where there is a strong Western Civilisation, there can be no platform for the likes of it.

---

2   Kuehnelt-Leddihn, E. von (1974). *Leftism: From de Sade and Marx to Hitler and Marcuse*, New York: Arlington House Publishers, p. 39.

Chapter 3

Democracy Isn't Working

THE LEFT LOVES DEMOCRACY, EXCEPT of course when things fail to go their way. Their juvenile failure to accept recent democratic results does not simply end by drowning in their tears: idle talk of impeachment has yet to relent since the, albeit somewhat disappointing, election of Trump in the US. Also, the left have campaigned vigorously for a second referendum on Brexit, despite its irrefutable economic benefit and the failure of any promised apocalypse to materialise. And examples of the rise of right-wing nationalism can be found now in Norway, Poland and Austria.

The young leftists' frustration is palpable as they run off to join the terror group, Antifa. Is it any surprise they readily resort to violence? After all, Lenin wrote of *the usefulness*, even the necessity of democracy in the establishment of a socialist utopia, so long as it was egalitarian. Surely, they can hardly wait and wish to hurry the fulfilment of prophecy along. What's more, if one has no concern for private property, one probably has far fewer qualms regarding the use of violence.

So, someone such as I, who cherishes private property, must be head over heels with democracy these days. Right? How wrong you are!

The *bien pensants*, as a whole, are so ingratiating when they not only defend democracy, but do so because 'the people can be trusted to make the right decisions'. Setting the majority of people aside for one moment (bless them), democracy is, even on paper, the worst political system there is. Churchill (also overrated) was wrong when he said that it was the worst, *except for all the others* — chortle, chortle. No, Aristotle was right — democracy is simply the corrupted form of a republic. With the rule of many, indeed the rule of a majority, there are greater and more plentiful opportunities for corruption.

As celebrated as it is, democracy pits every conceivable group against the other, destroying trust in whole nations, let alone communities. Classes are divided as the political class offer the working class more of what the middle class are producing, all the while introducing yet another competing group of immigrants to replace a now dependent working class in the labour force. At least if a king becomes corrupt, you can rightfully execute the tyrant; aristocrats can potentially hold others in check; but, democracy is the cancer of political corruption.

Here is a brief summary of how the modern liberal democracy functions: The masses are presented with a dramatic show in which the forces of red vs. blue battle for power, and this circus gives them the comfortable illusion that benevolence is triumphing in the form of their new leader — not really too different to ancient Mesopotamian coronation rituals, only a bit less metaphysically sophisticated. In reality, the red vs. blue display is simply an equilibrium which is reached between one party, which represents the interests of an incentivised dependent class somewhat more than the other, which seemingly represents wealthier corporations a bit more. This is the inexorable result of a system which can be abused by any and every interest group, so long as they have the money or represent a significant number of predictable zealots who will consistently provide votes no matter which way the blind blows.

Western democracies are no less rigged than roulette, and the house always wins; both sides have candidates whose expensive campaign trails have been bought and paid for in return for reciprocal back scratching once the wealthiest interest groups have 'their man' in office. This surely explains the phenomena of politicians dramatically arguing over tiny percentages of national debt as though their views differed significantly, or their being incapable of keeping all their campaign promises.

Ultimately, what makes democracy most dangerous is that there is no meritocracy to it. People have decision-making power by virtue of falling out of their mothers and not dying for eighteen years. We wouldn't wish to *employ* someone on those criteria alone, yet the overwhelming majority religiously swear by these criteria in politics, not just for themselves but for every country. And, well, if it's good enough for the overwhelming majority...

Bringing the zombified masses to question their beliefs about democracy is nigh impossible; and it is precisely for this reason that large-scale democracy is so destructive — people are simply too simple for democracy. For years, I have been trying to convince others of the truth of Prof. Hoppe's *Democracy: The God That Failed* — that such a system degenerates society by offering everyone, from the working to the political class, a quick grab of power or resources with no concern for the long-term, no thought for heritable interests etc. In that time, I have come to learn a lot about the general psychological condition of Westerners. I now understand why people won't change their minds about democracy and why granting them political responsibility is extremely *irresponsible* and promotes further irresponsibility.

Let's just look at three general psychological traits of the masses: low IQs, the Dunning-Kruger effect and Haidt's Elephant.

For whites/Europeans, the average IQ is 100.[1] Albeit, we have a greater representation among the gifted and intelligent than East Asians, whose average is several points higher overall. Sounds good, so what's the problem? It is a small, absolute minority which possesses IQs above 120, i.e. those who *can* gather and infer their own information, let alone the smaller group who actually *do*. With that in mind, we must look at the Dunning-Kruger effect: despite 'lack[ing] the mental tools needed to make meaningful judgments', as one study put it, people assume their mental abilities are greater than they are.[2]

More significantly, when they cannot grasp thinking which is above them, they assume the more intelligent are incompetent and trust instead in their own judgment. This renders the masses unable to select the best

---

1 See Rushton, J. P. (2000 ed.). *Race, Evolution and Behavior: A Life History Perspective*, Charles Darwin Research Institute.
2 Wolchover, N. (2012). 'People Aren't Smart Enough for Democracy to Flourish, Scientists Say'; https://www.livescience.com/18706-people-smart-democracy.html (27/10/2017).

representation and, worse, it makes them vulnerable to deception and exploitation by those smarter than themselves (perhaps one of several reasons democratic offices attract sociopaths).[3]

So, what can stir the masses from their slumber? Haidt's increasingly popular analogy of an elephant and its rider is a fine way of describing the political defensiveness we are all prone to. Our ideological baggage, especially in our subconscious, is the elephant we (hopefully, with some control) ride around on.[4] Overcoming this beast has to come from a gentle process of listening to others' beliefs, acknowledging shared aims and the good in their intent, thus, giving them the opportunity to be civil and to reciprocate. There is no guarantee they will change their views of course, but you stand a better chance than charging at them, on the offensive; the elephant will reel, the defences will go up and your views will be stubbornly dismissed.

On the large-scale, masses can be manipulated by the self-interested and sincere alike. In Le Bon's *The Crowd: A Study of the Popular Mind*, he noted typical traits of the mass mentality: 'impulsiveness, irritability, incapacity to reason, the absence of judgment and of the critical spirit, the exaggeration of the sentiments' etc. Hitler famously made good use of this understanding, swaying the black and white emotional thinking of the masses and completely curtailing Haidt's Elephant. Such a strategy is open to all and so I candidly employ it with you now.

We share the same wants and needs: security and freedom for ourselves and our loved ones, and the wherewithal to make enough money

---

3   'Yes, politicians are more likely than people in the general population to be sociopaths. I think you would find no expert in the field of sociopathy/psychopathy/antisocial personality disorder who would dispute this... That a small minority of human beings literally have no conscience was and is a bitter pill for our society to swallow — but it does explain a great many things, shamelessly deceitful political behavior being one.' — Dr. Martha Stout, author of *The Sociopath Next Door*, retrieved from: Freeman, D. (2012) 'Are Politicians Psychopaths'; https://www.huffingtonpost.com/david-freeman/are-politicians-psychopaths_b_1818648.html (27/10/2017).

4   See Haidt, J. (2006). *The Happiness Hypothesis: Putting Ancient Wisdom to the Test of Modern Science*, London: Random House.

for leisure and other personal goals. Now, we both need a society that's stable enough to make this a long-term reality.

Democracy is failing its citizens across the West, society is polarising, and the achievement of your goals in the future is becoming increasingly uncertain. No, 'we, the people' cannot realistically be trusted to make the right decisions. According to the almost millenarian religion of progressivism, everything will inevitably get better as time marches on. But, the modern liberal democracy is simply a return to failed ideas of the ancient Greco-Roman world; these were replaced with more libertarian and sustainable systems of government in the Middle Ages — not *vice versa*.

If we want a high trust society and a prosperous future, we must first humble ourselves and trust in the natural hierarchy of tradition — the old order of aristocracy. What trust can we have in a subversive political class who claim to represent us but instead emotionally manipulate us, serving their own ends and those of wealthy interest groups? Down with democracy, up with the *noblesse oblige*!

CHAPTER 4

Europeans Want Hungary, Not Sweden

SHOULD WE BE SURPRISED THAT the mainstream media has paid zero attention to poll figures showing that Europeans want an absolute immigration ban on Muslims? After all, the same mainstream media bashed Trump's correct analysis of the 'rapefugee crisis' in Sweden, trying to convince us that things were actually getting better for Swedes!

Where, for instance, was the coverage of Peter Springare — long-time senior investigator at the serious crimes division at the Örebro Police Department, who is now being investigated for hate speech after blowing the whistle on Swedish crime stats on social media? No, the traitors who hold the reins in media and politics aren't interested in heroes who would enlighten their people, let alone inspire any sense of identity. No wonder police in the UK were so fearful of accusations of racism that the Rotherham child sexual exploitation scandal occurred, as it is doubtless still occurring across the UK.

Here is yet another example of detrimental media silence, but one we can take courage from: Last month, the Royal Institute of International Affairs in London polled ten thousand Europeans in ten countries and found that the majority agreed with the statement, 'All further migration from mainly Muslim countries should be stopped.'[1] I was fully expecting

---

1 See the study, 'What Do Europeans Think About Muslim Immigration', from Chatham House; https://www.chathamhouse.org/expert/comment/what-do-europeans-think-about-muslim-immigration (27/10/2017).

these figures to play some major role in the mainstream conversation on immigration but, sadly, the ball was kicked into the long grass.

The most interesting result of this poll was that those who disagreed with the statement never rose above 32% and, even then, this was a relatively high result from Spain. On average then, the mainstream media can only hope to muster the support of around a fifth of Western populations; the majority would rather agree with policy ideas espoused by Hungary.

Hungary's Prime Minister has taken an increasingly anti-immigrant stance and has challenged EU quotas in court. Where the EU directs that states are expected to take in a certain number, Minister Janos Lazar says, 'We shall not take anyone in in Hungary [sic.], we do not need immigration in Hungary.' With its razor wire fencing and laws allowing for the physical removal of migrants as they enter, Hungary's government seems to be the polar opposite of Sweden's in many ways. Not least of all in terms of how it is admired by Europeans at large.

The cultural Marxist fake news outlets and the globalist political class would have us believe the West is filled with multiculturalists who have no longing for cultural preservation, no concern for how demographic change might affect the long-term stability of their country. The data, however, are screaming the opposite. They cultural Marxists and globalists are right; there is a subversive minority trying to spoil our countries. But *they* are that minority! The establishment holds up Sweden as a success, whereas most Europeans secretly want Hungary; so, where do we go from here?

Many would assume a hatred of the *other* is what I am calling for; perhaps they would think I am calling for violence or that secretly in my heart that is what I really want. Let me be clear: I have dear friends, colleagues and, yes, family who are Muslims; when I look at Sharia, I see a system which is in many ways similar to that of natural law, which prevailed during the Middle Ages of Christendom (which I very much admire and write in support of); I find many people from Muslim-majority countries to generally possess virtuous qualities, not just towards their own, but toward the stranger in need of hospitality, which I would like to see more of amongst my own people. Nevertheless, their core values do not comport with those of Europe and so it would be preferable for them to have their own communities with their own laws and their own separate civilisation.

The time has come and gone for the silent majority to recognise that we *are the majority* and that we stand by as wicked men waste our civilisation. These days, being considered right-wing in any way can make life very difficult for one at work and elsewhere — I understand. But, consider this: we have been living off the moral and civilisational bank of the Christian age for centuries and, in our bankruptcy, it has been replaced by various sects of progressivism more closely resembling Gnosticism. Still, we are left with a culture which is fundamentally incompatible with conservative Islam. I needn't bother listing the obvious reasons for this: attitudes to marriage, women, entertainment, individual liberty etc. etc. The fault of terrorism in our own nations, therefore, is not to be laid at the feet of Muslims.

We must look to our own spiritual poverty and understand how *this* has allowed a system to arise which wreaks havoc and carnage in the Middle East and then throws open our doors to all those who would flee it, regardless of the reason. I want the majority, who wish to refuse Muslims access to Europe, to look in the mirror and realise that the eschewing of corruption in our lands starts with each one of us. So, yes, keep yourself informed with alternative media, share statistics like the poll above to boost confidence in those who are awake to the facts, and be more vocal on social media and in your everyday life, as the opportunities arise. But you must start with fixing up your own heart, mind and soul.

Remember, we stand against a small, absolute minority of those in our countries who do not care for Western civilisation, and the accomplishments and wonders of European history. Where we take pride and pleasure, they only want to destroy, starting with us as a people. Hungary is seeking to welcome Europeans fleeing their own countries, trying 'to find the Europe they have lost in their homelands', as Prime Minister Orbán put it. But don't flee; make a stand today, shoulder-to-shoulder with the majority who would save European culture.

To conclude, consider Orbán's Christmas message of 2017 and consider where you stand:

> According to the Gospel of Saint Mark, Christ's second commandment is 'Love your neighbour as yourself.' There has been much talk of Christ's commandment in Europe nowadays. It is used to rebuke us for declaring ourselves to be Christian, while at the same time declaring that we do not want millions of people from other continents settling in Europe — and that we even refuse to let them in.
>
> But this commandment consists of two parts, and our accusers have forgotten the second part: we must love our neighbour, but we must also love ourselves. Loving ourselves also means accepting and protecting everything that embodies what we are and who we are. Loving ourselves means that we love our country, our nation, our family, Hungarian culture and European civilisation. …
>
> Culture is similar to the human body's immune system: as long as it is working properly, we do not even notice it. It becomes noticeable and important to us when it is weakened. When crosses are airbrushed from photographs, when people seek to remove the cross from a statue of Pope John Paul II, when they try to change how we celebrate our festivals, then every right-thinking European citizen bristles with anger. … Europe's immune system is being deliberately weakened. They do not want us to be who we are. They want us to become something which we do not want to be. They want us to mix together with peoples from another world and, so that the process will be smooth, they want us to change. By the light of Christmas candles we can clearly see that when they attack Christian culture they are also attempting to eliminate Europe.[2]

---

2 Orbán, V. (2017). 'We Europeans Are Christians'; http://www.theimaginative conservative.org/2017/12/viktor-orban-european-christian-christmas-address-2017.html (31/12/2017).

Chapter 5

Why the West Can't Unite Against Terrorism

I'VE NOTED TWO BASIC RESPONSES to terror attacks from my fellow Englishmen. I imagine these pitiable reactions must be the same across Europe but the matter has been more pronounced for me in light of the two recent terror attacks on what is still called English soil—the '2017 Manchester Arena Bombing' and the latest London Bridge attack. The two reactions are: 1. Deluded patriotism; and 2. New Age prayer. I want to convince you that both these impotent attempts at social unity are symptoms of a spiritual sickness which we can readily cure.

London can take it!

Just before the recent, disastrous UK general election, Prime Minister Theresa May called for us to 'reignite the British spirit'. Also, following the attack in Manchester, my contact in the Conservative Party posted a picture of St. Paul's Cathedral standing above a smoky, blitzed London. I believe the intention was to ride the ripple of nationalism which moved across the West this past year. His caption read, 'London can take it.' My first thought was not, 'If my child had been killed in the London Bridge attack, I'd throw him under a bus for such an insensitive comment.' Rather, I was shocked that he assumed there *was* any patriotism to tap into. Not only did British patriotism pass into fond memory with the empire's collapse, but all these things were themselves symptoms of a lack of sound social identity. And no amount of increasingly unmasculine James Bond films can fix this.

It goes without saying that May's campaign for office reignited nothing. Nevertheless, I can hear the rebuttals now; many are proud of the 'Lion of London Bridge' — a man who fought off the most recent attackers — as a healthy sign of British patriotism. Unsurprisingly, those who clamour for identity in all the wrong places would have us believe the man was filled with thoughts of Queen and Country as he leaped up to fend off the machete-wielding zealots. Yet, what initially caught the Lion's eye was the attacker wearing a rival football shirt. 'F**k you!' he shouted. 'I'm Millwall!' His passion emerged from his loyalty to *a sports team* — the most common, imitation source of identity in the West today. Before you try to kid yourself that this was merely incidental to his unending love of Britain, parliamentary democracy etc., just remember that these words could easily have been his last.

Integrate into what exactly?

It is sad to see Brits call for Muslim immigrants to make more of an effort to integrate — and then, when radicals physically attack our soulless society, we scramble around looking for something outside of our consumerism for them to integrate into. The realisation that we have absolutely nothing to offer people from other civilisations except for smartphones and a relatively superior market, leads us to the next common reaction of Brits to terrorist attacks — New Agey platitudes.

The morning after the Manchester attack, in particular, radio presenters were umming and ahhing as they clamoured for some transcendent, collective value system to appeal to — something by which to objectively condemn the attacks. There was none, and so they attempted instead to focus on the best of human nature, rather than the worst — the heroic men who acted on their protective instincts to help others.

Phrases such as, 'It's just all about the love and togetherness, you know?' were ubiquitous. The only thing missing was the hippy's vocative case — 'maaaaan.' The aptly named memorial 'One Love' concert presented the perfect, if undignified, opportunity for various musicians to virtue signal to the world how in tune they are with the great spirit of love, peace, togetherness, vegetables etc. Do you see? We have no unifying cultural institution through which to mourn collectively, and so even the misery of our decline is merchandised.

But there is still the search for something more; not just to unite us but provide a common conscience and identity, to secure our people against the threats we face from within and without. The appeals to emotion and the use of pseudo-spiritual language are all our soul-starved people are familiar with — the glancing understanding their 'friend who does yoga' has of the transcendent. And *this* is precisely why we are a dying and conquerable civilisation.

The Church is Eastern Europe and Eastern Europe is the Church

How else are we to explain Europe's indomitable civilisation being beset by barbarians at the gates and the plutocratic pursuit of political power? The answer is apparent to much of Eastern Europe; they have seen where the unstable forces of leftism lead them and have returned to the Church as that common transcendent system of higher cultural values which bound Europe together into a network of communities. This is why they stand strong and terror-free, boldly declaring their Christian identity and closed borders in the face of the EU taking Poland, Czechia and Hungary to court.

But, today, where is our sense of community? We pass silently by each other from home to work and back again, so that we may consume some empty, urban pleasure with a handful of friends or family (if we have bothered to reproduce) on the weekend. This is what we have been reduced to.

It is undisputed that we Europeans are prone to individualism. This is certainly an advantage when it is countered by voluntary, pro-social institutions which provide that sense of self-actualisation and self-transcendence which Maslow identified as the highest of our needs. But such things have died a slow death throughout the modern period. The Renaissance saw the greed of bankers fight for individual freedom from responsibility, in an attempt to evade the Church's moralising about the working man. After the papacy had been corrupted and Europe was in a much weakened state, the Reformation was transformed from a movement which questioned said corruption into one which subverted all spiritual authority. Lutheran individualism was an opportunity for a rising mercantile elite to privatise the conscience of all, turning the obligations of sovereigns into the centralised systems of coercive powers we call nation states — money, religion, law and other important institutions were seized.

Eventually man would come to question all authorities (except for the now unlimited state) until he detached himself from all those cultural authorities which help us identify our purpose. What else are we Westerners today other than mere economic units? Yet we fancy our lives to be so much more attractive than those of traditional communities, who have no less access to the precious commodities by which we seek to define ourselves. But when we become so weak that the state power of our own government finds *us* to be the path of least resistance, we would rather adopt the slave ethic of blaming Muslim communities for being too strong than take a look in the mirror.

Unlike them, we have no common conscience to define ourselves with any more. We have sought something other than the Church to do so — the superiority of our people (like Germany) or the vastness of our colonialism; and, even today, the PM would wish these charred embers of the razed Church were somehow reignited, if only for a moment's warmth, rather than to rebuild and return to the true meaning of that most important of edifices. That of course would once more impose obligation and responsibility on any who assumed a position of power.

Belloc saw this cultural collapse coming even before WWII:

> Thus a whole religion sustains modern England, the religion of patriotism. Destroy that in men by some heretical development, by 'excepting' the doctrine that a man's prime duty is towards the political society to which he belongs, and England, as we know it, would gradually cease and become something other.[1]

---

1 Belloc, H. (2015 ed.). *The Great Heresies*, Cavalier Books, p. 6.

Following the nihilism of the 1960s and our current social bankruptcy, will we continue to clutch at straws? Will we learn the lesson of Eastern Europe and elevate religion as an important cultural institution which promotes self-limitation and love, or continue resorting to the coercion of socialism? Solzhenitsyn noted, 'Untouched by the breath of God, unrestricted by human conscience, both capitalism and socialism are repulsive.'[2] It seems inescapable then: that which maintains the level of social cohesion which keeps Eastern Europe relatively free of terrorism, is the spirit summed up by Viktor Orbán — 'Europe and the European identity is rooted in Christianity'. So, where do we go from here?

For the good of the country and countrymen we sincerely love, it seems that we must return to the Church. I shall let Solzhenitsyn have the final word:

> We shall have to rise to a new height of vision, to a new level of life where our physical nature will not be cursed as in the Middle Ages, but, even more importantly, our spiritual being will not be trampled upon as in the Modern era.[3]

---

2   Interview with Joseph Pearce (2003) 'An Interview with Alexander Solzhenitsyn'; https://www.catholiceducation.org/en/culture/art/an-interview-with-alexander-solzhenitsyn.html (29/11/2017).

3   Solzhenitsyn, A. (1978). 'A World Split Apart', Harvard University Address; http://www.americanrhetoric.com/speeches/alexandersolzhenitsynharvard.htm (27/10/2017).

Chapter 6

The Correlation Between State Growth and Mass Irresponsibility

It is my firm belief that the state is the embodiment of collective irresponsibility and that, for this reason, it incentivises its own growth. Having to maintain a good reputation in a community can be hard work; but, we live in a time of declining birth rates and a growing nanny state — our communities have all but perished in the increasingly hostile environment brought by the growth of the state. Allow me to give you a personal example to illustrate.

Very recently, someone close to me had her Nursery School business ranked inadequate by the UK government childcare regulator, Ofsted, for the simple fact that the staff were not preparing reports to prevent the radicalisation of these 1–3 year olds. It beggars belief that I should have to point out that the business caters to mostly middle-class white folks of Western and Eastern European backgrounds (not what you would call a high terror threat area), especially when this lady's business has been described as an institution of the local community many times in the decades since it was first established. Nevertheless, because this lady finds using the internet a nightmare (and we all know how user-friendly local council websites and networks are), and because nothing is sent to her via post any more (to save the whales and all that), she was unaware of this government regulation designed to prevent toddlers from becoming suicide bombers or white supremacists. She was planning to retire soon;

yet the state, with this slap in her face, seems completely out of touch with the community she has provided a service to.

So, the questions naturally arise: How did we get to the point where businesses of *good faith* count for nothing? How did we reach the stage where the state can declare pillars of the community inadequate over bureaucratic minutiae? More importantly, why do the masses automatically look to the state to fix these local issues when it is the state that is creating an inhospitable environment for the very communities we sorely lack?

Once the state gets its foot in the door, that's it — game over! Give it the proverbial inch and it will eventually become a handsomely paid middleman for every conceivable human interaction. Many will say this is a good thing — even those readers who fancy themselves 'conservatives'. But this does nothing but incentivise a lack of responsibility: if the state will take the blame, pick up the pieces, protect me, etc., what need have I for a good reputation with my neighbours, my local contacts, customers, what have you? And it's not just that European tendency to individualism which is to blame for this development, it is the majority who *want* the greater irresponsibility which the state fosters (irresponsibility being its only fuel-source).

This is the downward spiral of Western civilisation. Since Luther's irresponsibility in the face of spiritual authority was seized upon by various Northern European plutocrats, the state emerged to monopolise and centralise systems of control over the people — national churches, national currencies etc. etc. Hobbes' Leviathan — above the law, *dictator of* the law and, thus, chiefly irresponsible — reared its monstrous head, only to grow to Godzilla-like proportions of societal destruction. Various liberalising European movements, whilst rightly demanding greater freedom for the people, nevertheless looked to Leviathan to provide it and so began the separation of the folk from every existing community institution and their replacement with a new god. 'Greater freedom' amounted to no more than greater irresponsibility from group expectations in one's local community. Now, the state is the only platform through which anyone can do and, increasingly, think anything.

The problem is, being so far removed from real, rational, personable, human interaction, the state simply seeks to impose more regulations on our interactions in order to avoid having to take responsibility for certain of its own failings. 'What a litigious society we live in!' Well, we have made the state the all-father, and like father, like son: our only motivation in an irresponsible society is to cover our arses. The simple reason being, the state is no more than the manifestation of collective irresponsibility — everyone passing the buck to everyone else, collectively, so that no *one* might take the blame, except in those circumstances that a scapegoat is needed to quash any troublesome matter which might require the public to think. It is our failure to take individual responsibility for our actions, for the safety and stability of our communities, which has caused the power-vacuum now filled with a torrent of state regulations. And, so, only strong, healthy communities can take the power back for our own good.

Yet, it isn't just leftists who feed the monster; they are not alone in their general desire for the state to use its irresponsibility to interfere in private affairs for selfish ends. So-called conservatives have long forgotten the belief that communities, built from the bottom up, are the answer to our many social woes. They too think that the state can impose some top-down solution to incentivise greater social cohesion, but all this does is store up greater state power for the day when Leviathan is so powerful that all dissent results in family members going missing in the night. In short, they believe they can wield the One Ring of Power and not *vice versa*.

If you think this is an exaggeration, just look at how those countries which have emerged from the dreadful ashes of the Soviet Union have sought to reinvigorate those institutions and communities which sought to limit state power. This battle for social stability is very real and you must pick a side — individual responsibility or collective irresponsibility. Instead of burying one's head in the sand and imagining a Marxist utopia on the one hand, or an equally illusory state which encourages communities full of highly responsible individuals on the other, start taking greater responsibility in your local area and demanding the same of others. Moreover, empowering the Church and other such voluntary institutions which seek to impose greater obligations, but not greater rights, for public offices would be a good start.

Recent books, such as HSH Prince Hans-Adam II of Liechtenstein's *The State in the Third Millennium*, and Rod Dreher's *The Benedict Option: A Strategy for Christians in a Post-Christian Nation*, present a realisation that the West is in decline and that radical decentralisation is the only way to circle the wagons, as it were, and defend our civilisation in the same manner and for the same reasons as St. Benedict, who established the monastic system across Europe. For further consideration, we can look to the successes of communities such as the Tipi Loschi community of San Benedetto del Tronto in Italy, or the unincorporated community of Ave Maria, Florida, in the US. Even successful micro-states geared towards libertarian values, such as the establishment of Liberland, in Eastern Europe, present examples of what is possible. But this organic growth starts from the bottom-up. Take back responsibility today!

Part Four

FAMILY

CHAPTER 1

Why Women Are the Unfairer Sex

A STUDY BY THE WELL-KNOWN PROFESSOR Robert Dunbar has shown 'a very striking sex difference between male and female friendships.'[1] In the few days since Dunbar gave a talk on the results, a number of articles have been written of the superficiality of male relationships; they focused on Dunbar's view that 'women clearly have much more intense close friendships...very like romantic relationships...if they break, they break catastrophically.' Men on the other hand are painted as frivolous — 'With guys it is out of sight out of mind. They just find four more guys to go drinking with.' But, do the findings really indicate that women are friendlier or more sociable than men?

Now, of course, feminists will tell you that masculinity is inevitably oppressive and abusive, especially of the more supposedly feminine qualities of love, gentleness and empathy. But, this misconception is totally unfair. As Gillette and Moore point out, in *King, Warrior, Magician, Lover: Rediscovering the Archetypes of the Mature Masculine*, oppressive forms of patriarchy are simply based on the same juvenile fear depicted in *Lord of the Flies*; the 'mature masculine' psychology, however, is 'marked by calm, compassion, clarity of vision, and generativity.'[2]

---

1   Quotes from the Annual Meeting of the American Association for the Advancement of Science (2017) in Boston.
2   Gillette, D. & Moore, R. (1991). *King, Warrior, Magician, Lover: Rediscovering the Archetypes of the Mature Masculine*, HarperCollins, p. 6.

Indeed, science seems to agree, not only that hell hath no fury like a woman scorned, but also that women seem predisposed to scorning. For instance, women tend to dominate the judgmental and feelings-based personality types in Myers-Briggs Type Indicator tests. Naturally, when it comes to maternity, evolution has favoured those women with greater maternal instincts, but this doesn't mean women are necessarily the more sociable sex; nor does it mean that men are cold, superficial loners.

Whilst men had to go out hunting and patrolling, working together and trusting each other, women did not. This explains why Dunbar found that men can readily welcome and be welcomed into new groups of males—'What held up their friendships was doing stuff together.' Women, however, had to compete with other women over the loyalty of the alphas to their brood. It is easy, therefore, to see how being 'bitchy' or 'catty' evolved to try to lower the reputation of other women in the group and, thus, level the playing field. Furthermore, it also explains Dunbar's finding that long-distance female relationships can be maintained simply by gossiping on the phone.

In the real world, oft forgotten by the left, men love spending time with their 'honour group', yet the actresses of *Sex and the City* could barely stand each other's company long enough to create a fictional replica for women. Certainly, the reason women have such intimate relationships built on deep trust and loyalty has nothing to do with being friendlier or less superficial than men. This doesn't make one sex better than the other, it just helps us understand what we are and why calling on women to simply *be less judgmental* of each other is both ignorant and useless.

Another study has concluded that women are 'more sensitive than men to social exclusion, and when they feel threatened by the prospect of being left out, a woman's first response may be to socially exclude a third party.'[3] So, because ostracism of any kind would have meant certain doom

---

3 Benenson J.F., Markovits H., Hultgren B., Nguyen T., Bullock G., Wrangham R. (2013). 'Social Exclusion: More Important to Human Females Than Males', *PLOS ONE* 8(2): e55851; https://doi.org/10.1371/journal.pone.0055851.

for oneself and one's progeny, females have evolved to be more cliquey, and those alliances they do form are very high trust and with strong expectations of loyalty. Thus, Dunbar's conclusion regarding their relationships' intensity—'if they break, they break catastrophically.'

Now, I love women. The best relationships in my life have been with women—my grandmother, my mother, my wife, my daughter. I don't want to imagine a world without mothers and daughters. But, equally, I love manliness. We already face a dearth of true masculinity in our time; twisting the findings of Dunbar's study to suit commonplace misandry in the mainstream media and academia is beyond unhelpful.

I think the time for apologising about, and even concealing, biological trends must end immediately, and the time for celebrating alpha males must commence. Men are the more social animal and the friendlier sex, but feminists want women to take all the credit, imagining a world of sugar and spice vs. slugs and snails and puppy dogs' tails.

The fact is that the masculinity deficit we face in the West is due in no short part to a mischaracterisation of men. Feminists have denigrated masculinity for decades and, ironically, produced a generation of men full of fear and shame, who readily descend into the very angry and abusive, Lord of the Flies-esque behaviour the feminists claim to oppose.

Our forefathers had it right. We need a return of honourable masculinity; we should be celebrating masculinity and femininity for what they are and pursuing their ideal forms. Bashing male relationships and exaggerating female ones is completely unfair — especially if women want a reputation as the fairer sex.

Chapter 2

Four Reasons My Housewife is Awesome

YES, I WROTE 'AWESOME'. I know the word is misused but I'm not exaggerating the excellence of having a housewife. The typical complaint today, of course, would have nothing to do with the superlative I used; rather, the fact that I had anything nice to say about motherhood and home-making at all. This pseudo-feminism, which currently strangles our beloved Western civilisation with a dead fallopian tube, preaches: move to the city; have a career; and screw around until your ovaries are borderline useless, because kids are yucky.

Most, whose biological clocks continue ticking, eventually realise they've aged worse than the men, and the only men still unmarried are either too nutty or too fruity, like the rejects from a box of chocolates. These women have lost a depressing amount of sexual marketplace value.

In short, modern women have been defrauded of the enjoyment of their natural impulses and greatest ability.

Yes, greatest! The stigma seeded by the state and propagated by the media is against the 'stay at home' mother who doesn't pursue the empty and unrealistic *Sex and the City* 'adventure'. 'Staying at home' is the last way I'd describe how bloody difficult it is; but the West is increasingly void of real men to stick up for the women who choose this path.

Today, the state can just pull up, milk their taxes from two cash-cows in every family (to prop up the runaway, Keynesian, consumerist economy), and no one is there to protect or lead. Moreover, all the women who must now work in order to get a mortgage help to enforce the taboo. They speak of our beloved housewives with such disdain and catty jealousy. All this is killing the West in no uncertain terms; in my father's generation, an average working class family could get a decent mortgage on a single wage and have hope for their children's future.

Thankfully, my wife and I decided to have our children in our 20s and pursue other ambitions later.

She is intelligent, qualified and capable of higher-earning, professional work. Furthermore, when it comes to housework she is not so much a domestic goddess as a lonely rural priest, riddled with doubt and hitting the sauce. So why on earth do I defend and even venerate my housewife?

1. She produced my babies.

Don't recoil at this cliché. Yes, even women in comas have popped out offspring. Furthermore, there are plenty of sub-intelligent *Untermenschen* giving breeding a bad name. But, unless you have children, you're probably still focused on finding your next lay, not understanding what your genetic programming is trying to do. Children are not only the greatest joy you can have, but they give you some investment in the tribe, a reason to behave with honour and maybe even pride in one's culture.

Baby-makers are super-precious and in need of defending and celebrating. If you love Western Civilisation and remain unaffected as you stand at the cliff-side of our dropping middle-class birth rates, don't stop to read *A Farewell to Alms*, just befriend and commit to a good woman, who respects men, and make some sweet love. Nature will take care of the rest. 'I can't find such a woman,' you say? When was the last time you went to church?

2. She is an emotional port in the storm of life.

Whereas I try to toughen up my kids by describing the harsher truths of reality, simply wiping away the tears and telling them they're fine, my wife is soft, and home-making keeps her that way. Even when the children aren't really crying, they know they can get affection from mother dearest. They know a mother's love — always affectionate and warm, even if there isn't perfect understanding or even if it's not entirely deserved. That maternal instinct is hugely powerful and important from an evolutionary perspective.

As well as ensuring that my son knows how to identify maternal care in a potential mate and to steer clear of the ice queens, this also provides us chaps with a friend who knows how to listen. Of course, women want their men to be strong, just as the whole world expects men to be tough; but if they have that maternal instinct, they become an occasional confidant to whom we can open up about our misgivings. This strengthens a marriage/pair-bond and keeps families together through the long human childhood. Most importantly, however, as a housewife, she is always around. If she's coming home late, exhausted and stressed out by work, the right moment never comes to have that supportive chat.

3. Her looks will fade, but her cooking will only get better.

The way to a man's heart is not just through his stomach; his penis is obviously the highway. But, as that road gets old, the traffic lights don't work so well and…potholes. Let's be honest: women worry that when their looks fade, the man will leave and (aside from the revenge, money and state welfare resulting from the modern divorce case) they're not going to lure another man with ease, even with the benefit of an ex's money. But, when she devotes more of her time to creating the joys of a home for us, this relieves any worries for the future. My wife makes some of my favourite meals and is getting better all the time. That's leverage! I am always making more of an emotional investment in the family environment. And she happily knows that I couldn't get the same anywhere else and that, even though we pass through rough patches, I'll stay.

4. She embraces her biological role, which makes me want to be manlier.

When a woman strives to be more feminine, it highlights the degree of masculinity in the man. Furthermore, when she finds joy in being a woman, making the nest and producing offspring, it makes me want to find joy in being a better man. But, what is a man? The more I discovered about this, the more I wanted of it. I came to realise that our masculine culture of honour has been replaced with one in which the state manages everything for us, including fatherhood. It was the veneration of the mother which brought me to venerate patriarchy and to recognise the instability of the foundations upon which Western Civilisation currently rests. As Fulton Sheen put it, 'To a great extent, the level of any civilization is the level of its womanhood.' The more we learn about ourselves, the better-equipped we will be to make lasting repairs to those loose foundations.

Chapter 3

How to Be a Good Father

At a time when many Western men don't even want to be a father, it may be considered out of touch to discuss the importance of pursuing its excellence. Moreover, my eldest of three children is still only five, so I must also contend with the accusation of pretence. But, I am an early years professional and the facts paint a clear picture that we can all recognise: we need the return of traditional families and patriarchy.

Now, don't expect the culturally Marxist establishment to help you out. The glue which holds the suicidal fragments of today's status quo together is their hatred of straight white men; you think they want more of you? Yet, the demographic Winter is coming, the signs are all there — Europeans breeding way below replacement levels, a runaway Keynesian economy, the ageing of the higher spending generation etc. etc. Your example as a father could stave off the worst of it for Western civilisation.

So, now that I have your attention, how can you be a good dad? Before we begin, self-reflection has been a precursor for obtaining wisdom in the rationalistic West since the age of heroes. Remember, the ancient Greeks had inscribed 'Know thyself' at the forecourt of their temples. What are your strengths and weaknesses? Are you cold and unempathetic around children and teens? Would you be exhausted after five minutes alone with them? None of these are impediments to fatherhood but you need to know what you can offer and what will take more practice.

You may likely have children that are similar to you or your wife and who are perfectly happy engaging in the activities you are, but they might be different, very different to anyone else. Once you know the tools you are working with and the nature of the child you are working on, reaching the level of *gong fu* in the art of fatherhood only requires good planning and flexibility. I would advise using Maslow's hierarchy of needs, a mainstay for early years educators, to create an action plan.

1. Physiological Needs

You remember the film *Gremlins*? There were three rules. Children are much easier — don't feed them after midnight is the only one of the three that applies. Air, food, water, clothing and shelter; if you're unable to provide these things in a developed country, that's probably because you are a child. Make sure everyone gets enough time outdoors, fruit and veg, and sleep — job done.

2. Safety Needs

Just keep everything up to waist height safe for their first three years (especially plug sockets and furniture corners). After that, accidents become a healthy part of their development; let them learn to risk assess for themselves. If they don't graze those knees and bump those heads, nature won't go easy on their retarded sense of caution.

On a serious note, don't harm your little ones out of anger. Punishment must always be handled as a matter of justice. As a father, you are the judge and the majority of studies have shown that disproportionate punishment, physical aggression and angry emotional outbursts have very damaging effects on human development. Not only will the child not learn about honour and justice, they will be much less able to control their temper and handle emotional situations with rationale for the rest of their lives. They will also pass on the same IQ-depleting, animalistic behaviour to their children, and so the vicious cycle continues. Revenge is a dish best served cold.

But, be warned! Children will drive you up the wall sometimes, just as the weaker sex often resorts to hurtful words, emotionally bullying us to do their will. Children have little to no baggage and are raw human emotion and instinct; as such, they can intuit and manipulate yours with ease, if you are suggestible enough, pointing out hypocrisies and pressing all the right buttons. You have to be as steel with them, cold and immovable, but when they genuinely need comfort, recognise it and open your heart to them. This way, they learn what good parenting looks like and the importance of being earnest, not just how to become a better liar for next time.

What's the best way to keep your own temper at bay? Financial security is the biggest cause of arguments and divorces etc., and the pressure is placed on the shoulders of men first, as the traditional hunter of the hunter-gatherers. Live within your means and try not to worry. Contrary to popular belief, children don't really need a lot and their education doesn't have to be too expensive if you're willing and able to spend more time with them yourself. Also, not every single person has to go to university and come out with debt and a useless degree.

3. Love and Belonging

Not to speak ill of homeschoolers, but letting your child out of the home to develop their own social groupings is just as important as the love they receive in the home. It is the other edge to the sword that is your child's social ability. If both are not kept sharp, then your child will be at a disadvantage in the real world.

Yes, out there, there are meanies who do not love and understand your child the way mumsy does, but that's the whole point. Iron sharpeneth iron and your child will need to learn the different characters and personalities out there, whom they want to befriend, whom they want to avoid and why.

We all need to belong to something. That's why even the most individualistic of libertarians will nevertheless join various groups and institutions. Alexis de Tocqueville thought the success of the American Republic as compared with the French was the churches which, although numerous in their denominations, bound the spirit of the Americans together across the country.

There's a reason that cultural and ethnic homogeneity are so crucial in the creation of high-trust societies. So, as a father, you have a duty to make sure your child grows up somewhere they belong in this most primal of ways. If having children doesn't give you the incentive to take an interest in politics and the society your child must inherit, I don't know what will.

As far as love in the home goes, you don't have to be gushing with emotion to let them know you love them. Routine, structure and stability are the greatest tokens of love for a child. Superficially, we can say that accepting them for who they are and kissing them goodnight are very healthy, but shaming them for being different to their brothers and sisters is bad, of course. Taking time for your children is at the heart of the matter.

Set times every week for family meetings, eat meals at least once a day together as a family with no distractions and have a board game evening, for instance. Make the home something that you are all collectively invested in and your child will know deep down that you want to be invested in them. Creating that platform gives them the space in which they can speak honestly with you about your parenting and genuinely listen to your parental wisdom in return.

4. Esteem

I'm at risk of repeating myself here. That's because children need to be out of the home and in an environment where they are not unconditionally loved in order to find out how they can earn the esteem of their peers and elders, as well as those whose opinions don't matter to them at all. But learn from the mistakes of the pushy parents who raise those over-competitive, ticking time-bombs we've all encountered. Studies show that children like this are more likely to reject you later in life and less likely to achieve a sense of fulfilment. Which leads us to self-actualisation.

5. Self-Actualisation

We all want our children to reach their fullest potential but, the trouble is, most of us are not really engaged in that task ourselves. Generally speaking, however, we want our children to succeed at something they love. The best way to do this is to understand what they're good at and play to their strengths, whilst supporting them in their weak areas.

For example, if yours are still young, study them to see what schemas they have. Schemas are the following psychological urges developed from their first year:

> ***Rotation*** — the love of things that spin or of simply being swung round;
>
> ***Trajectory*** — not just the joy of throwing things, but of making lines in space, even by dropping items from a height;
>
> ***Enveloping*** — housing my toys off in bricks always gave me a sense of security;
>
> ***Orientation*** — an interest in positioning oneself or objects in different ways, e.g. that satisfaction in turning the hourglass upside down;
>
> ***Positioning*** — for my son, the shapes must not only go in the correct hole but must be lined up perfectly for selection from the start;
>
> ***Connection*** — the love of building and dismantling bricks, train tracks etc.;
>
> ***Enclosure/Container*** — that fond memory of building a fort of sofa cushions can extend as far as insisting all your doodles have a border;
>
> ***Transporting*** — parents whose important items have been carried away by a dumper truck or train; and
>
> ***Transformation*** — the wonder of changing states and shapes, like melting ice.

Once you've got them sussed, thinking of toy ideas and study supports is much easier.

But, let's be honest, if your child isn't good at science, they probably won't be an astrophysicist and probably won't want to be; but that doesn't mean they shouldn't know how gravity works. If your child has a talent and they love a certain hobby, focus their energies on it and help them to excel; chances are, none of you will regret it or resent the other.

Transcendence

Interestingly, Maslow later revised self-actualisation. He thought it was aimless and without any end in sight, without some higher, transcendent goal. In the West, we have lost the concept of the *paterfamilias*, the father as both priest and king of the household, with the hearth keeping both the fire and name of the family alive, surrounded by statues and images of ancestors. The fireplace has been replaced by the television in most of our homes and the father has been replaced by the state in many more still.

As the priest of your family unit, your natural role is to act as a spiritual guide for your children, to the best of your knowledge and belief. Teach them the ways of your ancestors, about their culture and their role in the bigger picture. Teach them how to search within and without for answers, and how to respectfully disagree, so they do not end up mindlessly following authority.

In short, being a father is never going to be easy. Then again, nothing worth doing ever is. Become what you were born to be. But, if you're going to do it, do it right. You don't have to be the perfect father, you just have to keep at it. All cheesy clichés, yes? That's because these principles are time-honoured, tested and true. Let's keep it that way.

Chapter 4

Why Fighting Is Good for Men and Boys

What would you do if you saw two boys of six years wrestling? Their shirts off, red and sweaty, they have a large group of peers around them, cheering, eyes wide and knuckles white. Would you stop them, or give the young scraps some advice? Would you see a violent squabble, or boys acting on natural impulses which will better equip them to defend their family and neighbours later in life? The answer you give is, in large part, dependent on your gender; so, the fact that this scenario would make an increasingly large number of men upset is a sign of a collapsing civilisation. But, *nil desperandum*, Western civilisation has the solution!

As an early years professional, I saw education academics acknowledging the data — boys need 'rough and tumble' play for their mental and physical well-being. But they have no way of encouraging this in institutions where boys are immediately reprimanded for making finger-pistols at each other. Without saying it directly, they thought the majority female teaching staff for younger age ranges was pushing our boys' natural urge to fight like lion-cubs underground. What's more, the boys were made to feel bad about themselves and their very nature.

Their solution? They suggested that more men be encouraged to teach younger children and engage in rough play with them. Until the late 1800s, education was male dominated and boys spent a lot of time with male mentors. But, of course, there has been no effort to bring back that environment. Instead, a compromise between boys being boys and boys being fairy princesses was achieved — playing superheroes.

As though female teachers are going to tone down their disapproval as boys shoot lasers, magic and (Gaia forbid) bullets at each other. The treacherous political class present only feeble attempts to manage the symptoms of our societal masculinity problem — like sticking some tape over the burst pipe of our haemorrhaging testosterone as cultural Marxism continues to swing the pick-axe of nth-wave feminism at it. So, it's high time we took a few swings back.

But, first, we need to teach our lads how to fight.

At the age of six or seven, Viking children were taught the martial art of *Glima*. This was not just father and son play-fighting; boys and occasionally girls already wrestled with friends and family up to that age. This was more systematic, a group activity.

The Greeks also taught their boys how to wrestle, because our other ancestors could see the big picture. The Hoplites, for example, were individualistic free men of all ages who voluntarily came together to practice combat; this not only strengthened their communities but also allowed these farmers to fend off the Persian Empire. Yet today even isolated expressions of violence in computer games are questioned by SJWs. Nevertheless, all the signs are there — our boys are yearning for the same activities that were practised by their forefathers.

At college, I started an unofficial fight club — men only — based in large part on the book and movie of the same name, in which the narrator's Nietzschean alter ego, Tyler Durden, describes the bubbling frustration inside the ever-increasing number of 30-somethings coming together for underground fights: 'We're a generation of men raised by women.' Naturally, half the guys in my year were participating within a week. But, our young boys should be taught how to fight openly and without shame to avoid hidden expressions of violence and maybe even some mass-shootings by angry, young loners on medication. When they are young, it is the perfect time to teach them.

Young lads have no intention of seriously injuring their friends; it's just good fun and produces healthier attitudes towards violence, confidence in self-defence and the defence of one's community. Furthermore, the data show that fighting helps to strengthen peer relationships, meaning less bullying and segregation. It is interesting to compare the codes of honour of ancient Greek wrestling etc. with those we intuit as wrestling children.

No intentional hitting or kicking;
No gouging the eyes or biting; and
No going for the balls!

That's precisely how I used to wrestle with my brothers and friends as a pup; it was just obvious. If someone took things 'too far', they were ostracised from the fun, at least until they calmed down and apologised. If someone got hurt, we stopped, checked whether they were just being a pussy or needed mending. We kept calm and carried on.

The data are screaming that men haven't changed, especially in our need to practise fighting.

We still have the same natural impulses, but their suppression, no, their demonisation has made our men weak and submissive. So much so that many have become self-deprecating betas, full of white guilt and ashamed of Western civilisation, who believe that masculinity is toxic. We have everything to be *proud* of and need to encourage our boys' fighting spirit so they grow some balls, some confidence in themselves and their kin. That's the spirit which has kept our enemies, foreign and domestic at bay for thousands of years and will do the same to tyranny within and invading barbarians from without. If we want to turn scrapping boys into men first and gentlemen second, we need to organise some fights, not break them up.

ADDENDUM

Fifteen Steps to Restore the West

In the introduction of this book, I referred to Prof. Hoppe's speech, titled **'Libertarianism and the Alt-Right. In Search of a Libertarian Strategy for Social Change'**, delivered at the 12th annual meeting of the Property and Freedom Society in Bodrum, Turkey, on 17 September 2017. The body of his speech provides ten brilliant, albeit predominantly negative, steps to restore Western Civilisation. Below, are a summarised version of these ten 'specifics of a populist strategy for libertarian change' with the addition of my own five personal, positive steps:

Populist tactics

One: Stop mass immigration.

Two: Stop attacking, killing and bombing people in foreign countries.

Three: Defund the ruling elites and their intellectual bodyguards.

Four: End the FED and all central banks.

Five: Abolish all 'affirmative action' and 'non-discrimination' laws and regulations.

Six: Crush the 'Anti-Fascist' mob.

Seven: Crush the street criminals and gangs.

Eight: Get rid of all welfare parasites and bums.

Nine: Get the State out of education.

Personal tactics

Ten: Don't put your trust in politics or political parties.

Eleven: Affirm human free will and the consequent natural order of the human world, particularly one's natural rights.

Twelve: Promote individual responsibility in the local community from the family-outward.

Thirteen: Europeans, be proud of your identity, your traditions, heritage and culture, and defend these, especially by producing large well-developed families.

Fourteen: Repent and be baptised into the Church, defending and promoting your people's religion as opportunities arise.

Fifteen: Develop a skill set and otherwise prepare to establish possible segregated communities with like-minded folk, with the aim of preserving Western civilization.

AFTERWORD
Ricardo Duchesne

In this afterword I would like to reinforce Richard Storey's excellent effort to show that libertarian freedoms are not incompatible with a strong commitment to in-group white identity politics. Whether you prefer to call it 'libertarianism' or not, I fully agree with Storey that Europeans can preserve their freedoms only by living inside nations with a strong sense of ethnic, religious and historical identity.

The unique individualism of Europeans, including the liberal philosophy that came to justify it in the modern era, is now faulted for much that is wrong in the West today. It is said that liberalism prioritizes the abstract individual, regardless of race, nationality, religion and sexual orientation. Many on the Alt Right, followers of Alexander Dugin, to be sure, are calling for a Western world that is more in line with the way non-European societies are organized, with their authoritarian governments and strong collectivist values. But this is impossible. Europeans are innately individualist. This does not mean, however, that their liberalism inherently precludes them from recognizing the importance of collective identities, shared values and ancestries. Let us not forget that a few decades ago all the settler states of Canada, Australia, New Zealand, and America were full blown liberal states with strong collective identities that openly excluded non-European outsiders. These settler states, as well as the nations of Europe, were all conceived as nations with a strong ethnic identity, an identifiable territory, a language, myths and symbols, and common ethnic lineage.

At the same time, Carl Schmitt's assessment in the 1930s that liberal states have an inherently weak understanding of their collective political identity cannot be denied. European liberals wrongly imagine that their nation states were created through contractual arrangements by abstract individuals without deadly contests against outsiders and without a strong ethnic identity. Liberal theory has a progressivist inclination, or utopian hope, for a world in which all peoples will peacefully come together in pursuit of their natural right to life, liberty, and comfort. It imagines a world in which there will be no in-groups and no out-groups, in which the friend-enemy distinction, which Schmitt viewed as inherent to political relations between nations, will somehow vanish.

Having said this, it is important to make a distinction between the Anglo-American version of Western liberalism, which emphasizes 'negative liberty,' and the Germanic model of liberalism, which emphasizes 'positive liberty.' The Anglo version is more libertarian in focusing on individual agents and a 'minimalist' state that concentrates primarily on the security of individuals and their freedom to engage in contractual arrangements without obstacles or constraints imposed from above by state bureaucrats who think they know what is best for citizens. The Germanic version admires the heroic ethos of aristocratic freedom as well as the role of the state in encouraging the realization of one's highest potentialities. It accepts the value of negative freedoms — freedom of thought and assembly, equal treatment under the law — but without neglecting the fact that in the modern era individuals from different ethnic groups were coalesced into distinctive nations with shared collectivist values. The Germanic version recognizes that humans have a need to belong to a group or a *Volk*, and that the state is the one agent capable of ensuring this need. What Storey has endeavoured to show is that these two views of freedom are not necessarily opposed and that non-coercive systems of rulership have and could yet arise among European peoples.

Nevertheless, the German conception was once very influential in Europe and the United States, but after WWI and WWII this model was thoroughly discredited. Meanwhile, around the same time, the Anglo model came to embrace the notion of positive liberty (that the state should play a role in nurturing and sustaining the cohesiveness of the citizens making up the nation) from a leftist, Keynesian perspective, while still adhering to the principles of negative liberty. Among those associated with this Germanic conception, I would identify G. F. H. as the one thinker who offered the best argument reconciling the tendency among Europeans for individual liberty with the need humans have for communitarian values. Hegel, it seems to me, was the one thinker who recognized both the value of negative liberties and the need for shared values or for 'positive' freedoms.

Paleoconservatives, Traditionalists, Alain de Benoist and the European New Right, are wrong in condemning Western individualism and in calling for some return to ancient Greek ideals of 'social' freedom, or feudal 'organic' values, or for a 'traditionalism' that is inherently illiberal in the manner of non-Europeans. There is much to be learned from these schools in their emphasis on the natural inequalities of nature, their valuing of the Aristotelian virtues and the wisdom attained by past ages, and their respect for order and traditions. But there is no turning back from modern liberalism with its emphasis on separation of church and state, equality under the law, respect for private property and the privacy of individuals.

While I credit the prehistoric Indo-European aristocracies with originating individualism, and welcome the limitations imposed by feudal aristocracies against despotic powers throughout ancient and medieval times, White Identitarians should be wary of calling for a return of aristocratic rule in our modern age. We should welcome the political freedom and the equal rights of the *citoyens* sanctioned by the French Revolution. By modern times, the aristocracies of Europe had become parasitic courtiers, and were understandably replaced by bourgeois elites calling for representative institutions. After all, Storey's argument is that contemporary European nations should not accord superior rights and privileges to *any* European social class.

In my judgement, Hegel is the one modern thinker who offers the most adequate theoretical framework for the reconciliation of our individualism and our communitarian needs. The multicultural 'reconciliation' of the left was imposed from above by hostile elites against the natural prejudices of European peoples, against their own ways of life, their own communities, and their own (rationally approved) in-group preferences. The communitarianism of Hegel, however, recognizes i) the substantial unity of the traditional family, ii) the private sphere of markets and the world of civil society, in which individuals enjoy 'negative liberties' (private freedoms) to pursue their own lifestyle, as well as iii) a state, which expresses the general will and constitutes the sphere in charge of ensuring the 'social freedom' of citizens, legislation and execution in accord with the 'shared' values of the community, and constitutional liberal principles. Hegel specifically set out to solve the problem of how the growth of individuals who had subjected all traditional collectivities to the judgements of critical reason could create public institutions and a nation state that would make possible the central value of private freedom while ensuring that the nation would express the collective identity of the people and would embody their general will, the national interest of the citizens as a group.

There is no space here to enter a long textual disquisition into Hegel's political philosophy. Suffice it to say that Hegel's basic argument is that freedom has both a 'private,' subjective or 'libertarian' component, and a public, objective or collective component. Classical liberalism today tends to be defined by conservatives as free markets, formal equality before the law, and private enjoyment of life's goods. These private freedoms are known as 'negative liberties' in that they don't require anything from the public other than laws guaranteeing the security of private contracts and associations. The collective social freedoms are identified by leftists today with 'social rights,' equality of opportunity, welfare provisions, and the removal of all 'socially constructed' differences between men and women and races. Getting to the true aims of Hegel is very difficult because politically correct academics have forced ideas onto him that portray his collectivism in socialistic terms, at the same time that they have suppressed his rationally reflected traditionalism and nationalism. They have put forth a Hegel that views 'social rights' as rights for greater equality, a Hegel that synthesizes the atomism of free markets and private rights, with a state that ensures social rights for everyone and promotes the 'collective economic good' of society.

It is true that Hegel argued (correctly) that being recognized as a citizen while living in abject poverty was a violation of individual self-expression, insomuch as this was a result of the actions of powerful citizens having complete freedom of contract without any social rights protecting workers in the form of state regulation of working conditions. But there is a lot more to Hegel's concept of social freedom. When Hegel writes about a shared conception of the good, when he says that individuals enjoying their negative freedoms in the private sphere can be capable of embracing the social freedom of the state, meaning that they experience the ends of the state as integral to their own selfhood as modern rational citizens, he does not mean economic goods only; he means as well the cultural collective goods and sense of peoplehood (*Volk*) that can be guaranteed only by a national state. Hegel indeed appeals to the idea of national identity as the glue that can bind otherwise rational private citizens by virtue of their belonging, through birth and ethnicity, to a single culture.

Current interpreters of Hegel, notwithstanding the merits of their works in organizing and clarifying Hegel's extremely difficult ideas, either rarely mention or willfully misread Hegel's emphasis on national identity.[1] Frederick Neuhouser, for example, argues that Hegel could not have appealed to a sense of national belonging 'akin to bonds of brotherhood' since such bonds would be rooted in a 'pre-reflective attachment,' which is supposedly inconsistent with a post-Enlightenment culture in which individuals accept only communitarian identities that are 'consciously endorsed through a process of public reflection on the common good.'[2] Since it is a pervasive inclination of our times to argue that Western nations must be based on values alone, and since the dominant interpretation of Hegel today is that he was a liberal socialist, academics have happily

---

1 See Dominico Losurdo, *Hegel and the Freedom of the Moderns* (Duke University Press, 2004); Frederick Neuhouser, *Foundation of Hegel's Social Theory* (Harvard University Press, 2000); Fred Dallmayr, *G.W.F Hegel: Modernity and Politics* (SAGE Publications, 1993); and Shlomo Avineri, *Hegel's Theory of the Modern State* (Cambridge University Press, 1972).

2 Frederick Neuhouser, p. 138.

deluded themselves into believing that the act of consciously subjecting our laws, customs and beliefs to rational debate, seeking the approval of reason, automatically negates the actual biological realities of human bonding, 'the bonds of nature'.[3] But this is wishful thinking inconsistent with a free-thinking subject.

For starters, Neuhouser well knows that the 'bonds of love' that unite Western families are not purely 'free' and 'rational', even as the union of husband and wife was freely decided rather than coerced by unreflective customs. There is a strong natural bond between parents and children and between men and women as sexual beings who can reproduce children, not to mention the multiple customs that regulate the marriage ceremony and child-rearing. There is also, as Storey argues, a strong natural (but no longer pre-reflective) bond uniting people with the same historical ancestry, territorial roots, and language within one nation. This bond is consistent with a rationally free subject on two levels. Firstly, history teaches that those nations possessing a high degree of ethnic homogeneity, nations in which the ancestors of the present populace have lived for generations — England, France, Italy, Belgium, Holland, Sweden, Norway, Finland, and Denmark — were the ones with the strongest liberal traits, constitutions and institutions. Before immigration restrictions were eliminated starting in the 1960s, the very rationally oriented nation states of the West were reserved for people of similar ethnic and religious identities. Secondly, and contrary to our current juvenile misreading of Hegel, the subjection of 'pre-reflective bonds' to rational examination does not

---

3   One can appreciate that these Hegelian scholars were trying to correct the notion that Hegel was an illiberal advocate of Prussian authoritarian, anti-constitutional, and militaristic policies, a view most commonly associated with Karl Popper. But in trying to make Hegel palatable to a liberal establishment serving social democracy, the authors referenced here, among others, have taken it as a given, almost in a way similar to Popper, that liberal freedoms cannot co-exist with any form of ethnic nationalism, that a state with an ethnic identity amounts to chauvinistic nationalism and totalitarianism. The Canadian academic, John Russon, in Reading Hegel's Phenomenology (Indiana University Press, 2004), even tries to read into Hegel a call for Canada's multicultural state!

necessarily entail the cultural Marxist idea that everything is 'socially constructed' or that only 'propositional values' can be said to be acceptable as the uniting bonds of a nation. Thinking critically about 'pre-reflective bonds' means that these bonds can no longer be seen as unknowable, mysterious forces that control the affairs of men; it means that we now know their nature, that we can explain why individuals tend to be attached to people of their own ethnicity and historical lineage. It means that we have rationally explained studies about in-group attachments, biological dispositions, and genetic determinants.[4]

It means, finally, that we can see that leftist communitarians are deceivers, that the cosmopolitan universal values our current elites advocate are not rationally based, but have been concocted by rootless cosmopolitan academics and politicians engaged in the deliberate misreading of the great thinkers of the past to promote the insane idea that European ethnic identity is inherently violent and exclusionary, even though Europeans alone are responsible for modernity and even though there is now substantial evidence showing that humans are genetically inclined to prefer their own ethnic in-group and that diversity is coming with an incredible price in the form of systematic rapes, social disunity, suppression of rational debate, illiberal controls, and economic/environmental costs.

---

4 I am taking Hegelian reason as far as possible, while aware that we ultimately don't know why the universe exists in the first place; why there is being instead of nothing. There are limits to reason, but it is still the case that Europeans today can speak rationally about these limits and about what lies beyond reason.

BIBLIOGRAPHY

Augustine. *The City of God*. Ch. 4, 'How Like Kingdoms Without Justice are to Robberies'. http://www.newadvent.org/fathers/120104.htm (17/11/2017).

Belloc, H. (2015 ed.). *The Great Heresies*. Cavalier Books.

Benenson J. F., Markovits H., Hultgren B., Nguyen T., Bullock G., Wrangham R. (2013). 'Social Exclusion: More Important to Human Females Than Males'. *PLoS ONE*, 8(2): e55851. https://doi.org/10.1371/journal.pone.0055851.

Benson, B. L. (1990). *The Enterprise of Law: Justice Without the State*. Pacific Research Institute for Public Policy.

Berman, H. J. (1983). *Law and Revolution: The Formation of the Western Legal Tradition*. Harvard University Press.

Casey, G. (2012). *Libertarian Anarchy: Against the State*. Continuum International Publishing Group.

Clark, G. (2007). *A Farewell to Alms: A Brief Economic History of the World*. Princeton University Press.

Cochran, G. & Harpending, H. (2015). *10,000 Year Explosion: How Civilization Accelerated Human Evolution*. Basic Books.

Cox, D., Jones, R. P. & Navarro-Rivera, J. (2013). 'In Search of Libertarians in America'. PRRI. http://www.prri.org/research/2013-american-values-survey/ (29/12/2017)

Dawkins, R. (1989 ed.). *The Selfish Gene*. Oxford University Press, p. 3.

de Benoist, A. & Champetier, C. (2012). *Manifesto for a European Renaissance*. Arktos Media Ltd.

Diamond, J. (2005). *Guns, Germs, and Steel: The Fates of Human Societies*. W.W. Norton & Co.

Dreher, R. (2017). *The Benedict Option: A Strategy for Christians in a Post-Christian Nation*. Sentinel.

Duchesne, R. (2011). *The Uniqueness of Western Civilization*. Leiden: Brill.

———. (2013). 'Multicultural Historians: The Assault on Western Civilization and Defilement of the Historical Profession, Part I: Patrick O'Brien on the Scientific Revolution'. *The Occidental Quarterly*, 13, pp. 53–72.

———. (2015). 'The Greek-Roman Invention of Civic Identity versus the Current Demotion of European Ethnicity'. *The Occidental Quarterly*, 15.

———. (2017). 'Carl Schmitt Is Right: Liberal Nations Have Open Borders Because They Have No Concept of the Political'. *The Occidental Quarterly*, 17, pp. 35–45.

———. (2017). *Faustian Man in a Multicultural Age*. London: Arktos Media Ltd.

Ferguson, N. (2011). *Civilization: The West and the Rest*. Allen Lane.

Freeman, D. (2012). 'Are Politicians Psychopaths?' https://www.huffingtonpost.com/davidfreeman/are-politicians-psychopaths_b_1818648.html (27/10/2017).

Fukuyama, F. (2004). *State-Building: Governance and World Order in the Twenty-First Century*. London: Profile Books.

Gillette, D. & Moore, R. (1991). *King, Warrior, Magician, Lover: Rediscovering the Archetypes of the Mature Masculine*. HarperCollins.

Graf, K. 'Action-Based Jurisprudence: Praxeological Legal Theory in Relation to Economic Theory, Ethics, and Legal Practice'. *Libertarian Papers*, 3, 19 (2011).

Haidt, J. (2006). *The Happiness Hypothesis: Putting Ancient Wisdom to the Test of Modern Science*. London: Random House.

Hengel, M. (1980). *Jews, Greeks and Barbarians*. SCM Press.

———. (1989). *The 'Hellenization' of Judaea in the First Century After Christ*. SCM Press.

Herk, N. A., Schaubhut, N. A. & Thompson, R. C. (2009). 'Ethnic and Gender Differences in Best-Fit Type'. http://citeseerx.ist.psu.edu/viewdoc/download?doi=10.1.1.619.8867&rep=rep1&type=pdf (29/12/2017).

Hoppe, H. (1993). *The Economics and Ethics Of Private Property*. Boston: Kluwer Academic Publishers.

———. (2001). *Democracy — The God That Failed: The Economics and Politics of Monarchy, Democracy and Natural Order*. Transaction Publishers.

———. (2006). 'The Idea of a Private Law Society'. https://mises.org/library/idea-private-law-society (30/02/2016).

———. (2015). *A Short History of Man: Progress and Decline*. Alabama: Mises Institute.

———. (2017). 'Libertarianism and the Alt-Right. In Search of a Libertarian Strategy for Social Change'. Speech delivered at the 12th annual meeting of the Property and Freedom Society in Bodrum, Turkey, on September 17, 2017. https://misesuk.org/2017/10/20/libertarianism-and-the-alt-right-hoppe-speech-2017/ (29/12/2017).

Ignatiev, N. (2008). *One Summer Evening, When Race Becomes Real: Black and White Writers Confront Their Personal Histories*. SIU Press, p. 296.

Illing, S. (2017). 'Why social media is terrible for multiethnic democracies'. https://www.vox.com/policy-and-politics/2016/11/15/13593670/donald-trump-jonathan-haidt-social-media-polarization-europe-multiculturalism.

Iyer R., Koleva S., Graham J., Ditto P., Haidt J. (2012). 'Understanding Libertarian Morality: The Psychological Dispositions of Self-Identified Libertarians'. *PLoS ONE*, 7(8): e42366. https://doi.org/10.1371/journal.pone.0042366 (27/10/2017).

Jorjani, J. R. (2016). 'Rumi Was White'.

Kinsella, Stephan. 'Punishment and Proportionality: the Estoppel Approach'. *Journal of Libertarian Studies* 12, No. 1 (1996): 51, p. 3.

———. (1996). 'Libertarian theory of punishment and rights', *a. Loy. LAL Rev.*, 30.

Leoni, B. (1991). *Freedom and the Law*. Indianapolis: Liberty Fund Inc.

Lynn, R (2002). 'Racial and ethnic differences in psychopathic personality'. *Personality and Individual Differences*, 32, pp. 273–316.

Mercer, I. (2011). *Into the Cannibal's Pot: Lessons for America from Post-Apartheid South Africa*. Stairway Press.

Moody, R. (1993). '12 Psychological Type and Ethnicity: How Do Ethnographic and Type Descriptions Compare?' http://typeandculture.org/Pages/C_papers93/12MoodyHaw.pdf (27/10/2017).

Ober, J. (2015). *The Rise and Fall of Classical Greece*. Princeton University Press.

Obioma, C. (2016). 'There Are No Successful Black Nations'. https://foreignpolicy.com/2016/08/09/there-are-no-successful-black-nations-africa-diginty-racism-pan-africanism/ (11/11/2016).

Orban,V. (2017). 'We Europeans Are Christians'. http://www.theimaginativeconservative.org/2017/12/viktor-orban-european-christian-christmas-address-2017.html (31/12/2017).

Pearce, J. (2003). 'An Interview with Alexander Solzhenitsyn'. https://www.catholiceducation.org/en/culture/art/an-interview-with-alexander-solzhenitsyn.html (29/11/2017).

Peden, J. R. (2009). 'Inflation and the Fall of the Roman Empire'. https://mises.org/library/inflation-and-fall-roman-empire (11/05/2016).

Penman, J. (2015). *Biohistory*. Cambridge Scholars Publishing.

Pius, HSH Hans-Adam II (2009). *The State in the Third Millennium*. I.B. Tauris.

Qiuyan, Q. (2017). 'Chinese derogatory social media term for "white left" Western elites spreads'. http://www.globaltimes.cn/content/1047989.shtml (29/12/2017).

Rockwell, L. (2014). 'What Libertarianism Is, and Isn't'. https://www.lewrockwell.com/2014/03/lew-rockwell/what-libertarianism-is-and-isnt/ (29/10/2017).

Rothbard, M. (2002). *The Ethics of Liberty*. New York University Press.

———. (ed. 2014). 'A Libertarian View of Nationalism, Secession, and Ethnic Enclaves'. https://mises.org/blog/libertarian-view-nationalism-secession-and-ethnic-enclaves (29/10/2017).

Rushton, J. P. (2000 ed.). *Race, Evolution and Behavior: A Life History Perspective*. Charles Darwin Research Institute.

Salter, F. (2001). *Risky Transactions: Trust, Kinship and Ethnicity*. Berghahn Books.

———. (2006). *On Genetic Interests: Family, Ethnicity, and Humanity in an Age of Mass Migration*. Transaction Publishers.

Sanandaji, N. (2015). *Scandinavian Unexceptionalism*. The Institute of Economic Affairs.

Siedentop, L. (2014). *Inventing the Individual: The Origins of Western Liberalism*. Allen Lane.

Sinha, S. P. (1993). *Jurisprudence Legal Philosophy: In a Nutshell*. St. Paul, Minn.: West Pub. Co.

———. (1995). 'Non-Universality of Law'. *ARSP: Archiv Für Rechts- Und Sozialphilosophie / Archives for Philosophy of Law and Social Philosophy*, 81(2).

Solzhenitsyn, A. (1978). 'A World Split Apart'. Harvard University Address. http://www.americanrhetoric.com/speeches/alexandersolzhenitsynharvard.htm (27/10/2017).

Szmodis, J. (2011). 'On Law, History and Philosophy'. *Sectio Juridica et Politica*, Miskolc, Tomus XXIX/1.

———. (2005). 'Reality of the Law: from the Etruscan Religion to the Postmodern Theories of Law'. Budapest: Kairosz.
van Dun, F. (2003). 'Natural Law. A Logical Analysis'. *Etica & Politica / Ethics & Politics*, 2003, 2.
———. 'Argumentation Ethics and The Philosophy of Freedom'. *Libertarian Papers*, 1, 19 (2009).
———. 'Natural Law'. http://users.ugent.be/~frvandun/Texts/Logica/NaturalLaw.htm (28/10/2017).
———. 'Kritarchy'. https://americankritarchists.wordpress.com/article-by-frank-van-dun/ (29/10/2017).
von Kuehnelt-Leddihn, E. (1974). *Leftism: From de Sade and Marx to Hitler and Marcuse*. New York: Arlington House Publishers.
von Mises, L. (1998). *Human Action: Scholar's Edition*. Alabama: The Ludwig von Mises Institute.
———. (1957). *Theory and History*. New Haven: Yale University Press.
Wade, N. (2007). 'Origins of the Etruscans: Was Herodotus right?' *The New York Times*. http://www.nytimes.com/2007/04/03/health/03iht-snetrus.1.5127788.html?_r=0 (04/05/2016).
———. (2015). *A Troublesome Inheritance*. New York: Penguin Books.
Wolchover, N. (2012). 'People Aren't Smart Enough for Democracy to Flourish, Scientists Say'. https://www.livescience.com/18706-people-smart-democracy.html (27/10/2017).

INDEX

0–9
10,000 Year Explosion, The (Cochran and Harpending), 67
2017 Manchester Arena Bombing, 111–112

A
Aarhus University, 68
Abraham, 24
academia, 9
Achilles, 77
Acton, John Dalberg-, 17
Africa and Africans, 57–59, 61–66, 70, 78
Alexander the Great, 77
Alt Right, 141
America. *See* United States
Ananias, 24
Antifa, 102, 139
argumentation ethics, 29–30, 40
aristocracy, 11–12, 20, 70, 72, 78, 103, 106, 142–143
Aristotle, 18, 59, 71, 102, 143
Asia and Asians, 69–71, 74, 104. *See also* China; Japan
Augustine, Saint, 9, 17, 58
Australia, 141
Austria, 1, 102
Ave Maria, 119

B
baizuo, 88
Bantu, 57–58
Barbary Slave Trade. *See* slavery
Belgium, 1, 146
Belloc, Hilaire, 114
Benedict Option, The (Dreher), 119
Benedict, Saint, 119
Ben Sira, 24
Benson, Bruce L., 29, 72
Bible, 43
Biohistory: Decline and Fall of the West (Penman), 64

Black's Law Dictionary, 40
Blade Runner, 35
Block, Walter, 65
Brexit, 1, 102

C
Canada, 1, 141
Canon law. *See under* Catholic Church
Casey, Gerard, 19, 39
Catalonia, 1
Catholic Church, 37, 39, 41, 43–44, 72–75, 114, 118–119, 149. *See also* Christianity
  Canon law, 21, 33, 41
  College of Cardinals, 21
  natural law and, 10, 19–25
  West and, 37, 114
chastity, 64–65
children
  education and, 132, 135–137
  fighting and, 136–138
  needs of, 131–135
China and the Chinese, 59–60, 65, 70–71, 74, 78, 88, 96
Christ, Jesus, 22, 64, 83
Christendom. *See under* Christianity
Christianity, 1–2, 47, 86, 109–110. *See also* Catholicism
  Africa and, 63–64
  Christendom, 1–2, 19, 42–43, 62, 72, 75, 108
  Europe and, 22, 109–110, 113–115
  Hellenism and, 22
  Judaism and, 22
  natural law and, 19–25
  Protestantism, 43
  West and, 25, 37
Church. *See* Catholic Church
Churchill, Winston, 102
Cicero, 14
civil law. *See under* Europe
Clark, Gregory, 68

Cleopatra, 58
Cichran, Greg, 67
Cold Winters Theory, 69
College of Cardinals. See under Catholic Church
common law. See under law
Communism, 96
communitarianism, 144
conservatism, 117–118
consumerism, 126
Critique of Pure Reason (Kant), 57
Crowd: A Study of the Popular Mind, The (Le Bon), 105
cultural Marxism, 7, 35, 50, 88–89, 108, 130, 137, 146–147
Czechia, 113

D
Dark Age, 64
Darwin, Charles, 71
Dawkins, Richard, 86–87
de Benoist, Alain, 143
Deist, Jeff, 35–37, 42–43
democracy, 21, 50, 87–88, 100, 102–106
Democracy — The God That Failed (Hoppe), 36, 104
Denmark, 68, 146
Dialogue with Trypho the Jew (Justin), 24
Diamond, Jared, 67
Diaspora. See under Judaism
DiCaprio, Leonardo, 59
divorce, 128, 132
dominium, 74
Dreher, Rod, 119
Duchesne Ricardo, 1, 10–13, 19, 22, 49–50, 60, 70, 72–73, 78, 90, 95, 97
Dugin, Alexander, 141
Dunbar, Robert, 123–125
Dunning-Kruger effect, 104

E
Eastern Europe. See under Europe
education, 132, 140
egalitarianism, 7
Egypt, Ancient, 58
England, 111, 114, 146. See also London; United Kingdom

Enlightenment, 21–22, 43, 50–51, 96, 145
Enterprise of Law, The (Benson), 29
estoppel, 26–34, 40
ethny, 52–53
Etruscans, 14–15
Europe, 1, 35, 39, 50, 62, 95–98, 108–109, 119, 147. See also Middle Ages; West
Christianity and, 64, 113–115
Civil law of, 33, 72–73
demography and, 130
Eastern Europe, 113–115, 119
individualism and, 113–114, 117, 141
philosophy and, 60, 83, 141
psychology of, 80–84
rationality and, 71–72
European Union, 1, 108

F
Farewell to Alms, A (Clark), 69, 127
Fascism, 96
fatherhood, 129–135
Faust, 77, 82
Faustian spirit, 70–71, 74, 77–80, 82–83, 90, 99
feminism, 123, 125–126, 137
Ferguson, Niall, 67, 73
Fight Club, 137
Finland, 146
folk rights, 52–53
Foreign Policy, 61
France, 132, 146
Frankenstein, 77
Frankfurt school, 89
freedom. See liberty
French Revolution, 21, 143
friend-enemy distinction, 142

G
Galilei, Galileo, 71
gender, 67
Germany, 114
Ghana, 62
Gillette, Douglas, 123
Glima, 137
globalism, 108
Gnosticism, 109
Graf, Konrad, 28, 32, 41

Gramsci, Antonio, 89
Greece, Ancient, 7, 10–14, 22, 74, 83, 130, 143
  education and, 137–138
  individualism and, 11–12, 143
  Judaism and, 22–23
  natural law and, 10–14
Gregorian Reform, 21
Gregory VII (pope), 21
Guns, Germs, and Steel (Diamond), 67

H

Haidt, Jonathan, 73, 76, 105
Haidt's Elephant, 105–106
Hans-Adam II, 119
Harpending, Henry, 67
Harvard University, 85
Hávamál, 75
Hector, 77
Hegel, Georg Wilhelm Friedrich, 80, 143–147
Hellas. *See* Greece, Ancient
Hengel, Martin, 22–23
Heraclitus, 24
Herod, 23
Hitler, Adolf, 105
Hobbes, Thomas, 43–44, 117
Holland, 146
Homer, 11, 13
homosexuality, 68
Hoppe, Hans-Hermann, 2–3, 16, 20, 26–31, 33, 36, 40–42, 89–90, 104, 130
Hume, David, 39
Hume's law, 39
Hungary, 107–110, 113

I

identitarianism, 35
Ignatiev, Noel, 85
immigration, 2
imperialism, 95, 97
imperium, 74
individualism, 35–36, 43, 46, 89, 95, 113–114, 117, 143
Indo-Europeans, 1, 7–8, 10, 19, 90, 143
  aristocracy and, 20–21
  kingship and, 10, 12, 19–20
  liberty and, 12

international law. *See under* law
Into the Cannibal's Pot (Mercer), 65
Investiture Controversy, 21
IQ, 47, 65–66, 78, 104, 131
Islam and Muslims, 59, 71, 108–109, 112, 114
Israel, 23, 100
Italy, 146

J

Japan and the Japanese, 47, 52, 71, 78
Jerusalem, 22–24
Jesus. *See* Christ, Jesus
Jorjani, Jason Reza, 59
Judaism, 22–23
  Diaspora and, 24
  Hellanism and, 22–23
Jung, Carl, 79–81
jurisprudence, 38–40
  praxeological 26–34, 41
jus sanguinis, 51–52, 100
jus soli, 51
justice, 37, 39–41, 43, 131
Justin, Saint, 24

K

Kant, Immanuel, 57
Keirsey, David, 81–83
Kern, Fritz, 19
Keynesian economy, 100, 126, 130, 142–143
King, Warrior, Magician, Lover (Gillette and Moore), 123
kingship, 19–20, 74–75, 103
Kingship and Law in the Middle Ages (Kern), 19
Kinsella, Stephan, 28, 31, 40
Koheleth, 24
Korea, 78
Kuehnelt-Leddihn, Erik von, 45, 101

L

law, 7. *See also* natural law; positive law
  common, 40–41
  international, 41–42
  justice and, 41
  morality and, 8, 28–29

law (cont.):
  rule of, 8, 75
  violence and, 31, 33, 37–38
  West and, 72
  Lazar, Janos, 108
  Le Bon, Gustave, 105
  legal positivism. *See* positivism, legal
Leges Duodecim Tabularum, 15
Lenin, Vladimir
Leoni, Bruno, 15
liberalism, 50–51, 95–98, 103, 141–144
Liberia, 51
Liberland, 119
libertarianism, 1, 36–37, 132, 139
  aristocracy and, 70, 72, 142–143
  Catholic Church and, 44
  definition of, 7–8, 37
  ethics and, 7
  family and, 44
  identity politics and, 141–147
  individualism and, 35–36, 42, 132
  law and, 7, 38, 42–43
  liberalism and, 142–144
  multiculturalism and, 41, 46–47, 53
  nationalism and, 46–48
  natural law and, 1–2, 38, 44
  non-aggression principle and, 31
  psychopathy and, 70–71
  rights and, 31
  as theory of law, 7–8, 37
  values of, 1–2
  West and, 47, 52–53, 67–74, 106
liberty, 142–144
Locke, John, 33
London, 107, 111
London Bridge attack, 111
Lord Acton. *See* Acton, John Dalberg-
Lord of the Flies (Golding), 123
Lukács, György, 89
Luther, Martin, 114, 117
Lynn, Richard, 67–71, 78

M

Machiavelli, Niccolò, 43
Mark, Saint, 110
Marxism. *See* cultural Marxism
masculinity. *See* men
Maslow, Abraham, 135

Maslow's hierarchy of needs, 44, 113, 131, 135
May, Theresa, 111–112
McLintock, 74
media, 86, 89, 108, 125
Medieval Period. *See* Middle Ages
men, 123–124, 129
Mercer, Ilana, 65
meritocracy, 103
Merkel, Angela, 96
Middle Ages, 1, 19–20, 29, 35, 39, 41, 69, 72, 106, 108, 115
Mises, Ludwig von, 29
Mises Institute, 35
moderation, 13
Moody, Raymond, 80–82
Moore, Robert, 123
multiculturalism, 41, 46, 51, 53, 75, 87, 95, 101, 108, 133, 143, 147
Mycenaean Kingdom, 11
Myers-Briggs Type Indicator, 73, 81, 124

N

nationalism, 1, 46–53, 102, 111. *See also* nation-state
  civic vs. ethnic, 2
  immigration and, 2
  reasons for rise of, 2
  statism and, 46
nation-state, 21. *See also* nationalism
Naturalization Law (USA), 51
natural law, 2, 33–34, 37. *See also* law; positive law
  Christianity and, 19–25, 37
  definition of, 39–40
  divine law and, 39
  Enlightenment and, 43
  history of, 10–25
  Indo-Europeans and, 10–14
  praxeological jurisprudence and, 28, 41
  Romans and, 14–19
neoconservatives, 99–101
Neuhouser, Frederick, 145–146
New Right, 21–22, 143
New Testament, 24
New Zealand, 141
Nietzsche, Friedrich, 12, 74–75, 137
nihilism, 37

Nigeria, 61
non-aggression principle (NAP), 7–8, 31, 40
Nordic countries, 47
Norway, 102, 146
Nozick, Robert, 38
Nyborg, Helmuth, 68

O

Obioma, Chigozie, 61–63, 66
Odyssey (Homer), 13
Old Testament, 23–24
On Genetic Interests (Salter), 52
Orbán, Viktor, 108–110, 115
Ottoman Empire, 63

P

paleoconservatism, 143
Palestine, 23
Papal Revolution, 41
patriarchy, 130
Paul, Saint, 24
Peden, Joseph R., 16–17
Penman, Jim, 64, 66
personalism, 42–45
Pinker, Steve, 68
Philosophy of Mind (Hegel), 80
Plato, 14, 59, 71, 77, 81
Poland, 102, 113
political correctness, 67–68
political spectrum, 85, 96
positivism, legal, 28, 44. See also positive law
positive law, 18–19. See also law; natural law; positivism
praxeological jurisprudence. See under jurisprudence
Priam, 77
Prince, The (Machiavelli), 43
Private Governance (Stringham), 29
Prometheus, 77, 79, 82
Property and Freedom Society, 41
property rights. See under rights
property, private, 29–31, 38, 102
Property and Freedom Society, 139
Protestant Reformation, 21, 43–44, 114
Protestantism. See under Christianity
psychopathy, 68–69, 70–71, 78, 83, 87, 90

Ptolemy, 58

Q

Qur'an, 59

R

race, human, 52–53, 68, 85
Rand, Ayn, 42
Rawls, John, 38
Reformation. See Protestant Reformation
Renaissance, 22, 75, 77, 82–83, 113–114
right of blood. See *jus sanguinis*
right of soil. See *jus soli*
rights, 8, 27–28, 38
  property, 8, 28–30, 44
  universal, 10–11
Rockwell, Lew, 7, 37
Rome, Ancient, 14–19, 47
  civil law and, 14–15, 33
  natural law and, 14–19
Rothbard, M., 14, 35–36, 38–40, 46–47
Rotherham, 107
rule of law. See *under* law
Rumi, 59

S

Salter, Frank, 52
Salvian, 17
Sanandaji, Nima, 47
Scandinavian Unexceptionalism (Sanandaji), 47
Schmitt, Carl, 75, 141–142
Scholastics, 21
School of Oriental and African Studies (SOAS), 57, 60
Scruton, Sir Roger, 57
Selfish Gene, The (Dawkins), 86–87
self-ownership, 30
Sex and the City, 124, 126
Sharia, 108
Sheen, Fulton, 129
Simpsons, 43
Sinha, Surya P., 8–9, 11, 72
slavery, 61, 63
SOAS. See School of Oriental and African Studies
social contract, 44

social justice, 25, 38
Socrates, 24
Solzhenitsyn, Aleksandr, 115
South Korea, 62
Soviet Union, 118
Spain, 108
Spengler, Oswald, 71, 78, 80, 82
Springare, Peter, 107
Star Trek, 35
state
   definition of, 26
   effectiveness of, 67
   estoppel of, 26–34
   irrationality of, 26–27
   justice of, 27, 33
   power and, 33, 117
   responsibility and, 116–119
State in the Third Millennium, The (Hans-Adam II), 119
Stoicism, 24
Stringham, Edward P., 29
Sweden, 107–110, 146
Syria, 96
Szmodis, Jenő, 14–15

T

Taoism, 59–60
taxation, 32
temperance, 73–75
terrorism, 109, 111–115
testosterone, 68–69, 100
Thales of Miletus, 11
Thomas Aquinas, 40
time preference, 73–75
Tipi Loschi, 119
Tocqueville, Alexis de, 132
traditionalism, 2
Traditionalism, 143
Trump, Donald, 1, 96, 102, 107
Tutankhamun, 58

U

U.K. *See* United Kingdom
Uniqueness of Western Civilization, The (Duchesne), 60, 70, 78, 95
United Kingdom, 107, 116. *See also* England; London
United States, 1, 36, 51, 102, 132, 141–142
University of Ghent, 1

University of London, 57
University of New Brunswick, 1
University of Ulster, 67
U.S. *See* United States

V

van Dun, Frank, 1–2, 27, 39, 41, 45
Vikings, 137
violence, 7, 31, 33, 37–38, 40
virtue, 13
Visegrád countries, 1

W

Wayne, John, 74
Weber, Max, 71–72, 80
West, 1, 26–27. *See also* Europe
   Christianity and, 25, 37
   citizenship in, 49–53
   civilization of, 46–48, 72, 78, 99, 101, 109, 117, 127, 129, 136–137, 139–140
   decline of, 119, 129–130
   family and, 146
   fatherhood and, 130, 135
   Faustian spirit and and, 70–71
   future of, 2
   law and, 8–9
   liberty and, 12
   natural law and, 25, 34
   restoration of, 139–140
   time preference and, 73–75
   uniqueness of, 8–25, 60, 67–76, 80–84
   white guilt, 85–91, 95, 97
women
   family and, 126–129
   friendship and, 123–124
   maternity and, 124, 126–128
World War I, 142
World War II, 50, 114, 142

Y

Yoruba, 58–59

Z

Zionism
Zoroastrianism, 59

OTHER BOOKS PUBLISHED BY ARKTOS

Sri Dharma Pravartaka Acharya	*The Dharma Manifesto*
Joakim Andersen	*Rising from the Ruins: The Right of the 21st Century*
Alain de Benoist	*Beyond Human Rights*
	Carl Schmitt Today
	The Indo-Europeans
	Manifesto for a European Renaissance
	On the Brink of the Abyss
	The Problem of Democracy
	Runes and the Origins of Writing
	View from the Right (vol. 1–3)
Arthur Moeller van den Bruck	*Germany's Third Empire*
Matt Battaglioli	*The Consequences of Equality*
Kerry Bolton	*Revolution from Above*
	Yockey: A Fascist Odyssey
Isac Boman	*Money Power*
Ricardo Duchesne	*Faustian Man in a Multicultural Age*
Alexander Dugin	*Ethnos and Society*
	Eurasian Mission: An Introduction to Neo-Eurasianism
	The Fourth Political Theory
	Last War of the World-Island
	Putin vs Putin
	The Rise of the Fourth Political Theory
Mark Dyal	*Hated and Proud*
Koenraad Elst	*Return of the Swastika*
Julius Evola	*The Bow and the Club*
	Fascism Viewed from the Right
	A Handbook for Right-Wing Youth
	Metaphysics of War
	The Myth of the Blood
	Notes on the Third Reich
	The Path of Cinnabar
	Recognitions
	A Traditionalist Confronts Fascism
Guillaume Faye	*Archeofuturism*
	Archeofuturism 2.0
	The Colonisation of Europe
	Convergence of Catastrophes

OTHER BOOKS PUBLISHED BY ARKTOS

	A Global Coup
	Sex and Deviance
	Understanding Islam
	Why We Fight
Daniel S. Forrest	*Suprahumanism*
Andrew Fraser	*Dissident Dispatches*
	The WASP Question
Génération Identitaire	*We are Generation Identity*
Paul Gottfried	*War and Democracy*
Porus Homi Havewala	*The Saga of the Aryan Race*
Lars Holger Holm	*Hiding in Broad Daylight*
	Homo Maximus
	Incidents of Travel in Latin America
	The Owls of Afrasiab
Alexander Jacob	*De Naturae Natura*
Jason Reza Jorjani	*Prometheus and Atlas*
	World State of Emergency
Roderick Kaine	*Smart and SeXy*
Peter King	*Here and Now*
	Keeping Things Close
Ludwig Klages	*The Biocentric Worldview*
	Cosmogonic Reflections
Pierre Krebs	*Fighting for the Essence*
Stephen Pax Leonard	*Travels in Cultural Nihilism*
Pentti Linkola	*Can Life Prevail?*
H. P. Lovecraft	*The Conservative*
Charles Maurras	*The Future of the Intelligentsia & For a French Awakening*
Michael O'Meara	*Guillaume Faye and the Battle of Europe*
	New Culture, New Right
Brian Anse Patrick	*The NRA and the Media*
	Rise of the Anti-Media
	The Ten Commandments of Propaganda
	Zombology

OTHER BOOKS PUBLISHED BY ARKTOS

TITO PERDUE	*The Bent Pyramid*
	Morning Crafts
	Philip
	William's House (vol. 1–4)
RAIDO	*A Handbook of Traditional Living*
STEVEN J. ROSEN	*The Agni and the Ecstasy*
	The Jedi in the Lotus
RICHARD RUDGLEY	*Barbarians*
	Essential Substances
	Wildest Dreams
ERNST VON SALOMON	*It Cannot Be Stormed*
	The Outlaws
SRI SRI RAVI SHANKAR	*Celebrating Silence*
	Know Your Child
	Management Mantras
	Patanjali Yoga Sutras
	Secrets of Relationships
GEORGE T. SHAW (ED.)	*A Fair Hearing: The Alt-Right in the Words of Its Members and Leaders*
OSWALD SPENGLER	*Man and Technics*
TOMISLAV SUNIC	*Against Democracy and Equality*
	Homo Americanus
	Postmortem Report
	Titans are in Town
HANS-JÜRGEN SYBERBERG	*On the Fortunes and Misfortunes of Art in Post-War Germany*
ABIR TAHA	*Defining Terrorism: The End of Double Standards*
	The Epic of Arya (2nd ed.)
	Nietzsche's Coming God, or the Redemption of the Divine
	Verses of Light
BAL GANGADHAR TILAK	*The Arctic Home in the Vedas*
DOMINIQUE VENNER	*For a Positive Critique*
	The Shock of History
MARKUS WILLINGER	*A Europe of Nations*
	Generation Identity

Made in the USA
San Bernardino, CA
21 March 2019